Celia
Oct. 197

Celia Birtwell

by Celia Birtwell

Text by Dominic Lutyens

St. Martin's Griffin

For my lovely grandchildren:

Isabella, Scarlett, Tilly, Harry, Oscar, and Lola.

Thank you for keeping me constantly amused and on my toes.

When I was first asked if I wanted to compile a book about my life in design I was filled with trepidation. I have never enjoyed dwelling on or reminiscing about the past, so I have seen little point in it. I have always wanted to live in the present or look to the future. But at the same time I was honored and flattered that people might be interested enough in my work to warrant a book, so I put my feelings to one side and entered into the spirit of it.

For months and months I spent hours in glamorous tea rooms or at kitchen tables talking—first to my Publishers, and then to Dominic Lutyens—about my past. The process, while very cathartic, revealed many things to me: how fond and proud I am of my Northern roots—they shaped my attitude towards life and design; how much I loved art school and how it saved me by introducing me to like-minded people and allowing me to have lots of fun; that my life has been a patchwork of happy accidents without path or planning; and how hugely privileged I am that my prints have a language of their own that people really enjoy and understand.

However, what fills me with the greatest gratitude is the enduring support of my family and friends over the years; this has been the most important thing in my life. I want to thank them all: from Ossie, to whom I will be eternally grateful, and our sons Albert and George, to Brian Harris, Frances Lynn, Mo McDermott, Philip Prowse; and also, of course, Andrew Palmer, whose patience and love have been a continuous source of strength and encouragement to me. And, finally, I would like to say a special thank you to my dear friend David Hockney, who has been a constant fount of inspiration, amusement, and fun.

To readers, I would like to say that I hope you find some enjoyment within these pages.

Celia Birtwell

Right: *A fashion drawing produced by Celia Birtwell and Ossie Clark—their first collaboration.*
Title page: *David Hockney's 1972 crayon drawing* Celia in a Red and White Dress.

Celia
early days

Celia has very fond memories of her childhood. "I remember idyllic summer holidays spent every year, until I was about 10, at Beren in Denbighshire, north Wales," she recalls. "My parents, who'd spent their honeymoon there, were friends with a couple who had a farm with chickens and swallows. I have vivid memories of the house. It was lit by gaslight, and had a garden full of blue hydrangeas." The family holidayed there from Prestwich, near Manchester, where Celia (born in nearby Bury) was growing up; she was the eldest of three daughters—Diana (now deceased) was her middle sister, Caroline her youngest. "On our holidays, my father would go trout fishing. I remember watching him and the currents changing. We'd have picnics on the banks of the river, and go wading."

Celia's father was an estimating engineer at Mather & Platt, a manufacturer of textile machinery and fire extinguishers; her mother was a housewife who'd worked as a seamstress. "My parents had a very strong relationship," Celia says. "They were very sweet together. I remember GIs staying in the house; during the war, if you had a spare room you had to offer it to American GIs. My mother was very practical, my father was self-educated and loved art and literature. They were both Socialists, and my father was a conscientious objector and culturally curious. He was very bookish and loved art, particularly the French Impressionists. He had a print of a Degas painting of dancers above the fireplace. My father was always buying books—quietly—and putting up bookshelves. As he accumulated more books, they climbed the stairs, then seeped throughout the house."

Thanks to her father, too, nature had as much of an influence on Celia's childhood as culture: "My father loved his garden, and took great pride in his lawn. There was never much money but he was very inventive: he'd incorporate stones and wooden logs. My father's love of nature has definitely had a big influence on my designs. Life also revolved around school or playing out on the roads, which is practically unheard of now," she adds. "We played for hours in Heaton Park, a huge park in Prestwich, and made dens to play in."

Another early memory reveals Celia's mischievous streak: "I remember my Auntie Elsie's mahogany table. My mother had one of my sisters when I was five, so I was sent to stay with Auntie Elsie, a cousin

> *"My father's love of nature has definitely had a big influence on my textile designs."*

of my mother, and her daughter Janice. We'd sit at her dining-room table at mealtimes and she'd insist I eat the cabbage, which I hated. I'd stick it under the leaves of the table when she wasn't looking. She was a milliner, sang in the church choir, and was rather strict. I had to behave in a very proper way in her presence. But I remember drawing these figures, on that table of Auntie Elsie's." In fact, Celia began drawing and designing from a very young age, and showed an early talent for art.

Above, left to right: Celia in her grandparents' garden; in the front garden of her parents' home in Prestwich; with her mother; Celia's parents on honeymoon in Beren; her father at his desk at Mather & Platt in Oldham; her parents outside their home.

art school

At the unusually tender age of 13, Celia passed the exam to go to Salford Art School, where she studied textiles, lithography, and pottery. "I loved it. I thought, 'I've found my sort of people here.'" The school was part of Salford Technical College, in a Victorian building, and overlooked a Georgian crescent in an area called Peel Park. "We had an inspirational teacher called Frank Charlson. It was a varied course: we printed our own textiles in a rather crude way. But luckily that's what I decided to do as a career. We also did paintings with black lines in gouache or india ink, then put them under a tap so the paint would run—rather Jackson Pollock. Playing with chance and accidents was a big part of what we did. But our influences were mainly British and romantic—the art of Graham Sutherland and John Piper and Lucienne Day's abstract textiles. Local artist L. S. Lowry, who painted the Peel Park area, was another inspiration.

My mother was a big fan of his. I once saw him walking up some steps in Salford and thought he cut a solitary, mysterious figure. One of my best friends at art college was Roy Varndell, whose cousin—also a life model at the school—was Tony Warren, creator of (soap opera) *Coronation Street*." Another student and friend of Celia's was Brian Morris, now a production designer for films such as *Evita*. Celia also went out with a graphic design student named Sam Bernstein.

Celia then met her best friend at college, the late Mo McDermott, an artist. "Mo was part-time at the art school, and studied Egyptology at Salford Museum," she says. "He was gregarious, a true beatnik. We'd all been brought up in a formal way but Mo had a naughty, try-anything-once attitude. We'd go to Manchester's Cona coffee bar, which was very popular with students. He took purple hearts (a stimulant) and went to Manchester clubs: these were full of degenerates usually wearing black oilskin raincoats; the girls wore white lipstick and had Dusty Springfield

hairdos." And in the home of the parents of fellow student Lee Travis, "A crowd of us including Mo, Roy, Margaret Collins, Brian and I drank cider and danced to music on a wind-up gramophone in the cellar, fantasizing we were in a smoky Parisian beatnik club.

"At college at lunchtimes, Margaret, my partner in crime, and I would smoke in the lavatories. As we were economizing, we'd puff on half a cigarette —Woodbines or Players sold in a paper cornet not a rectangular packet—which we called 'dimps.' Once a week, we were allowed to dance in a common room —we'd dance to Bill Haley's 'Rock Around the Clock.' We'd also go to a lunchtime club held at the Odeon in Manchester where Jimmy Savile DJ-ed."

At art school, aged about 15, Celia remembers wearing a cream Burberry-style mac, as did Margaret, her best girlfriend. "It was our look and we'd defiantly wear them at all times, indoors and out. I'd also coax my mother to make the latest must-haves for me. We'd go to look at a Jacques Fath dress, say, in Kendall's,

Opposite, clockwise from top left: *Celia at primary school, second from left, first seated row; with cousin Janice; with Janice and Aunt Elsie; Celia (center) at a Whit Week walk (Whitsuntide celebrations).*
Above, left to right: *Celia in Peel Park in her Burberry raincoat; with her beau Sam Bernstein; rock climbing in the Yorkshire Dales.*

Manchester's smartest shop which sold French designers, then she'd go home and create a pattern. I hated sewing, I was too impatient, but I'd watch my mother for hours."

Celia's creativity at this age manifested itself particularly in interiors. "When my parents were away, I'd rejig the sitting room, fill it with Victorian paraphernalia like paraffin lamps and beaded footstools bought from junkshops, and invite friends round," she says. "I would buy old chemist's bottles, fill them with colored water and line them up in front of the windows so a jewel-like light would shine through."

meeting ossie

In 1959, she met the 16-year-old fledgling fashion designer Ossie Clark in the Cona coffee bar. Mo had moved to study at the Regional College of Art in Manchester with Ossie. "Mo said, 'There's this really

mad boy you should meet,'" Celia remembers. "Ossie was handsome, talented, lively but easily bored. He dressed in the style the Beatles were soon to adopt: moptop haircut, leather waistcoat cut into a V at the front, shirt with a rounded collar, and winkle-pickers (pointed-toe shoes). He looked very stylish."

Born in Liverpool in 1942 into a working-class family, Ossie was the youngest of six children. Originally named Raymond, he was nicknamed Ossie after Oswaldtwistle, the Lancashire village where the family had been evacuated during the war. His mother and sister Beryl were both very good knitters, particularly of Fair Isles, which Ossie wore as a child and as an adult. "My mother took a shine to him," says Celia. "She thought he had a real talent. He'd bring his homework and she'd show him how to put a collar or sleeve properly

Left: *L. S. Lowry's* "By the County Court, Salford" *(1926).*
Below left: *The majolica bust made by Celia.*
Below: *A sepia pen drawing by Celia of herself and her sisters.*
Opposite, from top to bottom: *Celia in Victorian clothing at Salford Museum; two illustrations by Celia done for her thesis.*

"I once saw Lowry walking up some steps in Salford and thought he cut a solitary, mysterious figure."

onto the rest of a garment.' Fashion writer Linda Watson says, "One of Ossie's earliest memories was of going to Celia's home and seeing those bottles filled with colored water." Celia also visited him at his home in Warrington, Cheshire. "Quite a few of his family were living there," she remembers. "When one of his sisters divorced and moved back, Ossie had to sleep on a chest of drawers on the staircase. The family were all talented in their various ways: his sister Kay was a jazz singer."

Celia's interest in fashion led to her doing a national diploma in textile design. She wrote her thesis—in immaculate italic script—on Victorian dress, illustrating it with drawings of crinolined women. Although the textiles she was designing were modernist in style, as were her clothes, her taste was beginning to take inspiration from Victorian design. "Even my hair went from being straight to curlier, more ringlety," she remembers. "I was partly influenced by memories of learning to play the piano in a Victorian interior in Prestwich. At college I made a majolica bust of a woman with ringlety, Victorian hair and started collecting Victoriana." At one point, Celia took part in a re-creation of a Victorian scene—"a sort of fashion show"—staged at Salford Museum, dressed as a Victorian lady.

After this, Celia's friends began moving out of Salford. 'I was teaching at my old college and was miserable that my friends had all left. But one day a girlfriend, Valerie Cunliffe, who'd moved to London, said, "Why don't you come here for the summer holidays?"; and Celia did. She found London so exciting—"it was 'Wow, this is where I want to be!'"—and felt she could never return to the North. In 1961, Celia moved permanently to London, where she and Ossie would soon be feted as two of Britain's most promising young designers.

celia hits london

Celia moved to the Notting Hill/ Ladbroke Grove area. It was yet to be gentrified, but by the early '60s an arty set was starting to colonize it. Celia put down roots, and she is still based there today. "I came to London before Ossie and Mo," she says. "They were dead jealous. Then Mo came down, followed by Ossie, who started studying at the Royal College of Art (in 1962)." Celia eventually rented a room on Addison Road in a house whose landlord was antique dealer John Manasseh. "John was very flamboyant," says Celia. "He wore astrakhan coats and drove a silver Studebaker. He had exquisite taste, and took me to antiques auctions in the country—an education in itself. My room had a French daybed with a twiddly ironwork frame and a Victorian screen."

Addison Road was full of eccentrics and colorful R. C. A. students, including artist Derek Boshier, and formidable

Above: *John Manasseh, antique dealer and landlord of Celia's home in Addison Road.*
Left: *Pauline Boty in front of her 1963 painting,* Celia and Her Heroes.
Below: *The invitation for a joint exhibition of work by artists Boty, Peter Blake, Christine Porter and Geoffrey Reeve; held in November 1961 at A.I.A. gallery in London it was hailed as one of the first British Pop Art shows.*
Opposite: *A Sonia Delaunay-inspired, early design by Celia for a fashion fabric.*

"Wow, this is where I want to be!"

BLAKE BOTY PORTER REEVE

theatrical costumier Doreen Brown. Also living there was the pop artist Pauline Boty, who died of cancer aged 28 and who is most famous for her 1963 painting of Marilyn Monroe, "The Only Blonde in the World." There were many parties. "We were beatniks in a ne'er-do-well house, paying only £2.50 to £5 a week for a room. I remember getting completely drunk on Cointreau once and everyone being sick on the rush matting!" she recalls.

"It was intimidating sharing a house with all these R. C. A. people," she says. At Henneky's, a local pub, Celia met many other R. C. A. students, including Peter Blake, Peter Phillips, and textile designer Natalie Gibson. "I think they saw me as a little oik from the North and thought they were the cat's whiskers. I suppose I did, too." In 1963, Boty painted the portrait "Celia and Her Heroes," in which Celia looks the picture of bohemian modernity in an unbuttoned shirt revealing a lacy bra and unkempt Bardot-esque hair, pictures of her idols, including Elvis Presley, David Hockney (whom she hadn't yet met), Marlon Brando, Hailie Selassie, and Alain Delon pinned on the wall behind her. "Pauline was iconic," says Celia. "She features big-time in Ken Russell's 1962 film on British Pop Art, *Pop Goes the Easel*."

wigs and waitressing

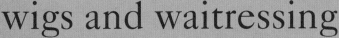

Celia had a string of jobs. "I worked in a soup kitchen then waitressed at a restaurant but was given the push 'for discourtesy.'" She was then a seamstress for Doreen Brown, through whom she met her long-term friend the director and stage designer Philip Prowse, who remembers her then as being coquettish and fashionably Francophile: "I met Celia when I was sitting with the awful Doreen in the back garden at Addison Road and this blonde girl—Celia—bounced in, bringing a phone message," he recalls. "Then she ran back into the house, and I said, 'She's rather nice,' but Doreen said, 'You need to watch her, she's trouble.' Celia was how girls wanted to look then: small, rounded, blonde."

Celia also worked at the very camp "Wig Creations," whose celebrity clients included Shirley Bassey. She got the sack for "being unkempt." "In fact I was wearing Foale and Tuffin clothes which I thought were chic," says Celia. "I was PA to a guy who I

suspected was a closet toupee-wearer." She then became a wig dresser at London's Aldywch Theatre and later for the Royal Shakespeare Company. "While at the RSC I met film costumier Anthony Powell and artist Hugh McKinnon, who asked me about my background. When I told them it was textile design, they said, 'Why aren't you doing that now?' I said, 'I have to make a living.' But on the strength of their encouragement, I went on the dole and produced some furnishing fabrics. I designed two slightly Op Art-inspired spotty fabrics for Heal's."

Around then, Celia vividly remembers seeing an exhibition on Diaghilev's Ballets Russes: "It was wonderful: the show was sprayed in Diaghilev's favorite scent, Mitsouko, by Guerlain." In fact, Leon Bakst's costumes for the Ballets Russes—which Celia pored over at the Victoria & Albert museum—and photos of Nijinksy were seminal influences on her early textiles.

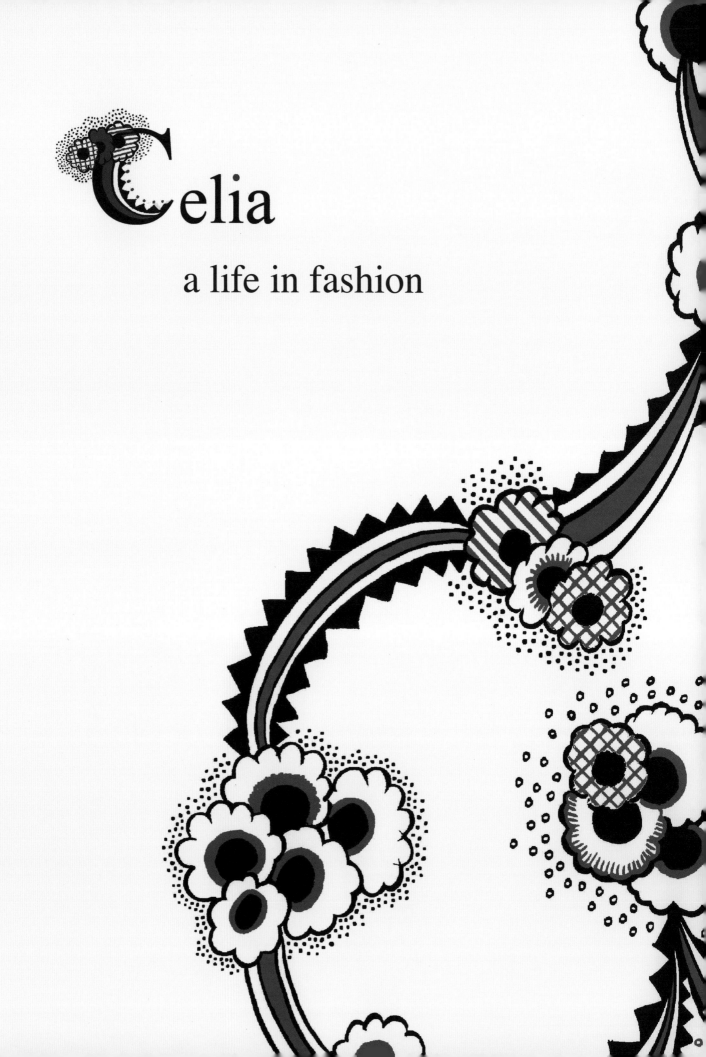

Celia

a life in fashion

celia & ossie

Celia began to see Ossie Clark while he was studying at the R. C. A. "He used to come to Addison Road, and he'd say, 'Can I stay?' I resisted at first," remembers Celia. "Philip and Pauline warned me against him. They said I was walking into something that would be very difficult, which it was. But Ossie was very persistent, and he won me over. I was attracted to his style and talent. Around this time, I had to move out of Addison Road and Ossie offered me refuge in his room above a bicycle shop on Westbourne Grove."

Ossie was soon being recognized as a new talent: in his second year at the R. C. A., he won a prize for a *Sunday Times* fashion competition, and in his final year, British *Vogue* featured him (in its August 1965 issue) beside a model wearing an outfit made of an Op Art-inspired fabric, shot by David Bailey. While at the R. C. A., Ossie had been taught by the legendary, visionary Janey Ironside, who once said of him:

"He was obviously very gifted from the beginning. His designs were already shadowing the 1930s and '40s."

Ossie's retro aesthetic was ahead of its time for presaging the softer, slinkier silhouette of '70s fashion, and Celia was on this wavelength, according to her friend, the milliner Brian Harris, whom she has known since the early '60s: "Celia's drawings were always nice and loose as opposed to the hard quality of '60s fashion. Her prints are soft and extremely pretty."

According to Norman Bain, a fellow R. C. A. student with Ossie, "a big influence on Ossie and Celia, and their taste for '30s-influenced bias-cut day dresses, was the 1939 film *The Women*, whose stars all wore clothes by legendary Hollywood costume designer Adrian. We also loved Mae West. Ossie, Celia and I would talk to each other imitating her voice for ages." "Ossie and Celia also liked Hollywood costume designer Travis Banton and Jean Harlow's films," says Harris.

Early on in their relationship, Celia and Ossie—who had previously done work experience at Christian Dior—traveled to Paris together. A highlight of the trip was a visit to the Chanel boutique on the rue Cambon, where they were invited to watch a client at a final fitting and glimpsed Coco herself on the fabulously mirrored staircase. But even at the start of their relationship, there was friction between the couple. "Around 1964 or '65, I went on holiday for six weeks to Greece with Mo, my first holiday abroad," says Celia. "I was trying to escape Ossie because we'd been having a difficult time. When I got back, Ossie kept phoning me. He said he wanted to get back with me. I said to him that it wasn't working but he had enormous persuasive charm and he finally moved in." By that time Celia had moved to St. Quintin Avenue, North Kensington. The couple had a white cat named Blanche and a black poodle named Beulah, after Mae West's line, in the movie *I'm No Angel*, "Beulah, peel me a grape."

quorum

Helping to precipitate Ossie and Celia's collaboration as designers was a chance encounter between Ossie and the designer Alice Pollock, who had a small boutique called Quorum in Ansdell Street, near High Street Kensington, which she opened in 1964 (and which moved in 1966 to Radnor Walk, off the King's Road). Ossie, a firm believer in astrology, felt that he and Alice were "twins" because they were born on the same day of the same month of the same year. Ossie joined the boutique as a designer and partner in 1965, and, soon after, Pollock asked Celia to design a fabric collection. Early Celia designs for Pollock included two border prints—one Cubist-inspired and one with

Celia and Ossie photographed by their friend Norman Bain in front of one of their first designs—a paper dress commissioned in 1967 by Molly Parkin, fashion editor of Nova *magazine (and shown on page 35). Celia remembers that "Ossie and I were into wearing tight Shetland sweaters bought from the shop Westaway & Westaway opposite the British Museum. I was also into knee socks I'd bought in Paris."*

tulips which climbed up the dress from the hem—and a "Sonia Delaunay and Bakst inspired" print of concentric circles in navy and white on organza. Ossie fashioned Celia's print into what she calls a "Bakst dress." It was photographed at the time on a rather stiffly posed model with a stylized topknot. "It was just before the hippie style kicked off and people were starting to let their hair down," comments Celia.

Her working partnership with Ossie, which was relaxed and marked by total freedom, anticipated this transition point in the mid-'60s when British society became less regimented. The collaboration also kickstarted Celia's habit of filling her sketchbooks with her inimitable, charming, color-drenched fashion sketches, whose romantic faces, with Cupid's-bow lips and haloes of curls, so resembled her own. "I'd ask Ossie which sketches he liked best, but he said, 'Do what you like,'" she says. "He thought it was my department. He trusted me implicitly."

brand-new craze for vintage clothing took off in the late '60s. On one foray to Portobello Market, Ossie bought a '30s dress and began experimenting with the bias cut. And he was a fan of 20th-century fashion designer Charles James (1906–78), famous for his shapely, highly structured clothes and use of the bias cut. Ossie and Celia were giving the diaphanous styles of the '30s a democratic twist, rather than mindlessly replicating the past. "The whole glamour thing of the 30s is what influenced us," said Ossie in a lecture in 1996. "But whereas in the '30s and '40s satin bias-cut dresses, feather boas and lace were worn by goddesses of the screen, we thought, 'Why can't people in the street wear them?'" "Ossie's style was 'old clothes made new,' but like Celia's fabrics they didn't mirror history, they were as modern as could be," recalls Harris, who created hats for one of the duo's fashion shows at the London club Revolution.

One reason for the modern spin Ossie put on these retro influences was the store he set by comfort: "For a garment to be successful it's got to flatter and be comfortable," he said in the

modern retro

In 1965, Ossie and Celia began renting one floor in a house in Blenheim Crescent, close to Portobello Road, which overlooked a Carmelite convent. At the time they loved trawling through Portobello Market, buying flowers, LPs (Ossie was a huge fan of contemporary pop and rock), crockery, and '20s, '30s, and '40s clothes with Art Deco and floral prints. Although 1930s floral prints were a major inspiration to Celia in the early '70s, when the '20s and '30s were enjoying a huge revival, she never based her flower patterns on them. Instead, her floral prints grew out of her own direct observation of flowers. "I drew straight from nature, drawing the flowers in a vase on my work table," she says.

Pioneered by the likes of Celia and Ossie, the

same 1996 lecture. Some believe that this stemmed from his being attracted to women (in addition to men) and to his having an intimate knowledge of their bodies. "My theory on Ossie's brilliance is that it was, in part, a consequence of his bisexuality," says fashion writer Linda Watson. "He understood a woman's body in a way not many men can. He saw them as

Top: *A late '60s fashion sketch by Celia. The girl's luxuriant long hair signals a change of mood from the stiff, stylized look of mid-60s fashion (see opposite) to the more relaxed hippie style of the late '60s and early '70s.*
Above: *A label on a Celia/Ossie dress featuring her print Pineapple.*
Opposite: *An early Sonia Delaunay, and Leon Bakst inspired print designed by Celia which Ossie fashioned into their "Bakst dress."*

goddesses—as many gay designers do—but also intimately understood a woman's anatomy. His dresses were sensual, never vulgar or crude. They were man magnets. The fact that women could totally relax in them was at the core of this. 'Comfort. That's the most important thing,' Ossie told me." Some, however, felt that comfort wasn't such a great concern for Ossie. "He often made sleeves which were too tight," says Celia. Even so, Ossie's tendency, from the late '60s, to cut his dresses on the bias meant they also suited a fuller figure.

Ossie's clothes began to look more retro and fluid by about 1967; that year he and Celia began to use ultra-romantic chiffons. Around this time, Ossie designed a jersey and organza dress apparently cut on the bias and began dropping his hemlines—a self-conscious and rebellious move. In 1967, in an article in *Nova*, the intelligent, hip women's magazine of the day, Ossie advocated "long skirts", which encouraged designers to "rethink the top half." "People will start looking at faces again instead of legs," he declaimed. Ossie could have been talking about Celia's fashion sketches, whose linchpins are their faces. That year, he was credited with introducing the midi-skirt, which was dubbed his "Bonnie and Clyde look", after the below-the-knee pencil skirts worn by Faye Dunaway in the hit movie, which also came out in 1967. Ossie's hemlines dropped even farther soon after, with his designs for maxi-skirts and leather maxi-coats.

Important influences for Celia's designs in the late '60s and early '70s were chinoiserie, japonaiserie, and kimono shapes. Celia knew Ossie had been introduced to, as she puts it, "the wonderful rooms of Oriental ceramics on the top floor of the V&A," and she too was interested in it. One Celia print of 1968 in yellow, black and cerise (also used for a scarf) incorporated a checkerboard pattern and stylized Japanese-inspired waves. And her illustration for it featured a girl with a sharply geometric, very Japanese-looking black bob.

But Celia was immersing herself in all sorts of cultures. Her prints nevertheless evolved gradually, with new designs often retaining elements from previous ones: her Greek Symphony print—inspired by Leon Bakst's costumes for the Ballets Russes—also incorporated the aforementioned checkerboard pattern and a new ivy motif.

celia's prints

The starting point for Celia's prints was always her fashion illustrations. "I'd usually sketch in the evenings at home on a work table in my bedroom. I loved doing it and found it very therapeutic."

"I'd invariably start with the girl's face then work down. If the face didn't have the right personality, I didn't carry on."

Celia bought her sketchbooks from a shop called Lamleys, in South Kensington "run by a very deaf old gentleman." "The books were lovely: the pages were like tissue paper but very strong." Once Celia had done several of her brilliantly, richly colorful felt-tip drawings, she chose the ones she liked best. "I would then blow up my prints to life-size which I would take to Ivo Printers, the London printer who screenprinted all my textiles, under the supervision of Ellen Haas.

"On average I used three colors per print, and I always chose the fabrics."

These tended to have a retro, luxurious appeal: georgette, silk chiffon, crepe-de-chine, voile, different weights of fabric. I soon became known for using transparent fabrics."

"I often advised Celia on the scale of her prints," says Ellen Haas, who set up Ivo in 1963 and began working with Celia around 1965. "If you print on a fine fabric, you can't have big areas of pigment as the fabric becomes too stiff." The mathematically gifted Haas also helped Celia to translate her drawings into precise repeat patterns.

Opposite and right: *Two late '60s sketches inspired by chinoiserie, japonaiserie, and kimono shapes—Celia was influenced by visits to the Oriental art rooms at the V&A.*

"Their clothes had an informality yet were
beautifully structured by Ossie."

Opposite: *Celia with her cat Blanche in her workroom at Linden Gardens, Notting Hill. The billowing chinoiserie-inspired scarf is printed with the same design as that on the trousers of her and Ossie's lamborghini suit.*
Above: *Amanda Lear modeling a silk-satin chinoiserie-inspired print by Celia on an Ossie trouser suit worn with a matching scarf.*

"Ossie and Celia's clothes were not well behaved, they were renegade, really rebellious."

Left: *Model Pattie Boyd, wearing a top featuring Celia's Greek Symphony print, with her then boyfriend, George Harrison. The print was inspired by Leon Bakst's costumes for the Ballets Russes.*
Above: *A dress with the print Flower Check, photographed by David Montgomery for* Vogue.
Right: *Ossie at home in Linden Gardens with the same dress, pictured above, behind him.*

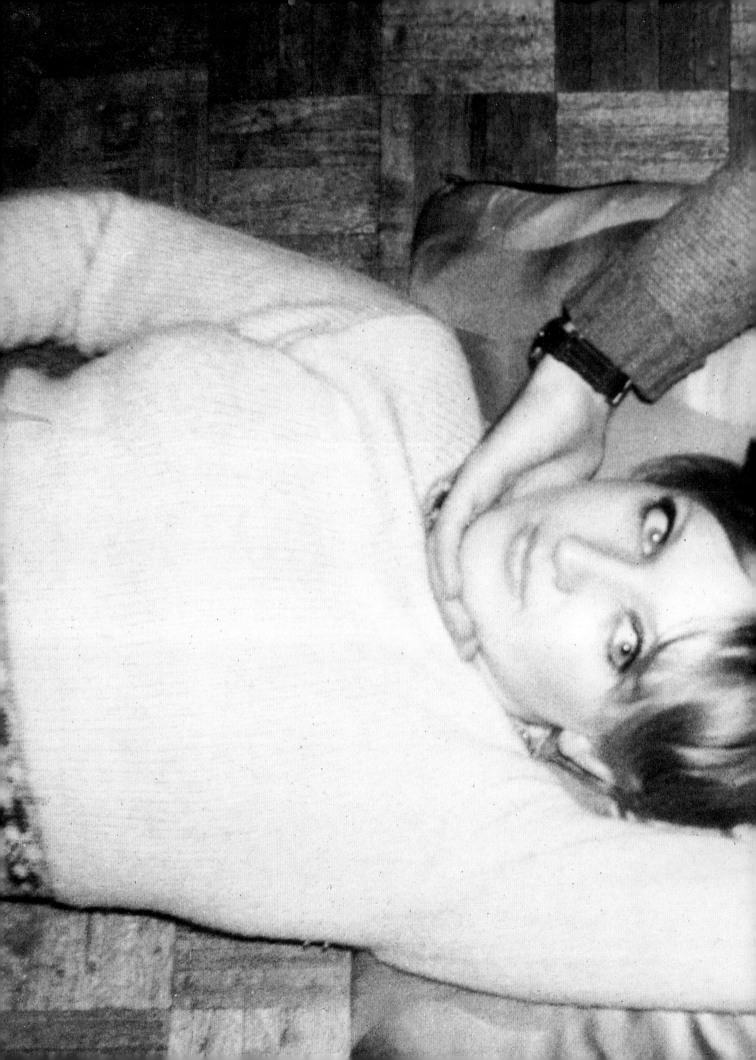

Celia, meanwhile, mixed color instinctively, deciding at the printers which colors worked well together. "Once Celia was satisfied with each color, the way it had been mixed was recorded with a recipe so it could be remixed exactly in the event of a reprint," says Haas. "If a different fabric was used, we tested the recipe on the new fabric to make sure the pigment printed equally well on it."

their chemistry

The closeness of Celia and Ossie's partnership was captured early on in an evocative photograph by their friend Norman Bain. "We'd go to Norman's place in Putney regularly," remembers Celia. "He had a very modern, smart apartment with parquet floors." "I took pictures of them one evening," recalls Bain. 'In one of them, they lay on the floor, resting their heads on purple and gold cushions from the '30s which they both really liked. When they came round Ossie would read any magazine lying around—he loved fashion magazines. He had an elfin charm. I'd go nearly every Saturday night to their home in Blenheim Crescent. I remember Ossie always listening to music. He had very good taste, and loved Dusty Springfield. Celia would spend a lot of time inserting swatches of fake hair into her fluffy blonde hair to build it up. As she knew how to dress wigs, she could sculpt her hair into all sorts of shapes. We'd often party in Notting Hill. When you saw them designing, the scene was almost too perfect. Ossie would be designing at one table, Celia at another. "They worked together in a totally organic way. You know how people say that couples finish each others' sentences. They would finish each other's designs. Celia has an amazing color sense. She has the ability to put together colors that no one else would think of putting together. Ossie didn't want to use anyone else's prints."

"With Ossie and Celia there was an unbelievable chemistry because you had—for the first and only time—a fashion and textile designer working in complete harmony," says Linda Watson. "Most textile designers don't think about where the print will end up, how it will work in three dimensions, but Celia always does. She would design the print and Ossie would play with the proportions. Both thought in three dimensions." Vanessa Denza, fashion consultant, agrees: "Celia always anticipates how her prints will look in 3D, they're not just seen as flat designs."

Many believe that Ossie's creations would have been far less sensational without Celia's input: "Ossie's dresses are well-cut, fit beautifully. But what makes them is the prints," says Brian Harris. "Essentially Celia chose the colors, and color is the most important thing in fashion." "Celia's prints were truly beautiful and there was nothing like them available," says Kathleen Coleman, Ossie and Celia's sample machinist, who was based at Quorum. "Ossie always

> ## "Most textile designers don't think about where the print will end up, how it will work in three dimensions, but Celia always does."

Previous pages: *Celia and Ossie photographed by Norman Bain in 1967 at his apartment in Putney, London.*

Right: *Celia's sketch of her print Roumanian Dancer.*
Far right: *Celia seen working at Linden Gardens in the film A Bigger Splash.*

 wanted to look at Celia's sketchbooks which really inspired him. He'd then look at his sketches and her prints, and decide which prints matched up with his designs best, sometimes adjusting his original designs in the process. Ossie and Celia had similar ideas about silhouette, but Ossie liked straighter, more tailored lines. He liked the strong, architectural line of a bib or yoke, softened, below the waistline, by a fuller shape created by panels or sunray pleats. The pleated skirts would sometimes be made out of a semicircle of fabric. As soon as they were made, we'd coil them around a hanger for a week, then let them drop so the pleats were sharper. This voluminous quality meant that women with fuller figures could wear his dresses as they adapted easily to different figures and were forgiving. Ossie was very aware of a woman's anatomy as a designer."

Many people say that Celia's practical streak was essential to the collaboration. Gregarious, mercurial, and hedonistic, Ossie was often out partying till dawn, while Celia was at home working or looking after their children: "Celia drove Ossie. Not only was she his muse, but she helped him to focus," says Brian Harris.

33

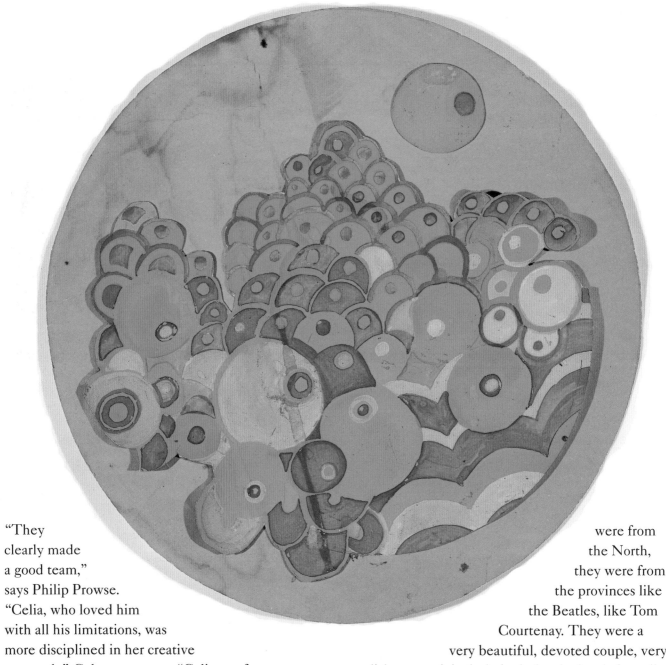

"They clearly made a good team," says Philip Prowse. "Celia, who loved him with all his limitations, was more disciplined in her creative approach." Coleman agrees: "Celia was far more disciplined and was so clever. It's a shame that Ossie got more of the fame. It was Celia who was the driving force. I don't think Ossie would have got so far without Celia."

Influential fans of the duo's earliest collaborative designs included fashion editors Prudence Glynn of *The* (London) *Times* and Molly Parkin of *Nova*. "I'd met Ossie and Celia at a party at David Hockney's," remembers Parkin. "To me, they represented a very modern way of living: Ossie was clearly gay, and yet he was in a relationship with Celia. Hockney seemed in love with Ossie and Celia. I liked that Celia and Ossie were from the North, they were from the provinces like the Beatles, like Tom Courtenay. They were a very beautiful, devoted couple, very stylish, very original; their clothes had an informality yet were beautifully structured by Ossie. They were not conformist; Ossie and Celia's clothes were not well-behaved, they were renegade, really rebellious."

Others have said the same: "There was a defiance to Celia and Ossie's clothes," says Prowse. "They made their own rules. The fact they came from the North meant they had a detached view of the British Establishment. In the 60s society was reorganizing itself—especially in London. In fact, Ossie and Celia hugely benefited from the energy of London and it's unlikely they could have done what they did without being there."

In 1967, Parkin commissioned them to create a mail-order paper dress for *Nova*. Shot by Duffy, the mini-dress was modeled by a young, Titian-haired Jane Asher posing in a super-Pop '60s interior. The dresses, sold for five shillings. "Ossie and Celia's youth perfectly exemplified the teenage stage of womanhood I wanted to illustrate," says Parkin. "Ossie had this Peter Pan look which would also prove ephemeral. As I associated youth with a throwaway attitude that things are temporary, expendable—like the working girls of the time who bought a new dress every Saturday, wore it that night, then binned it—so I filled the set, a mock-up of a bedsit (studio apartment), with furniture and objects made of paper, cardboard, and bright plastics. Even Jane Asher represented youth and transience. All attention was turned to her at the time: her boyfriend was Paul McCartney. For the dress, as part of the throwaway theme, I investigated using paper, and found one used by Johnson & Johnson for making J-cloths (cleaning cloths). The ink printed really well on the paper. The idea was very popular and spread like wildfire."

"We were flattered that Molly approached us," remembers Celia. "My initial designs for the paper dress, in gouache on paper, were inspired by the work of Paul Poiret and illustrations from (the stylish '20s fashion magazine) *Gazette du Bon Ton*. The company of Zika Ascher, who had printed artists' scarves for Picasso and Henry Moore, printed the dresses."

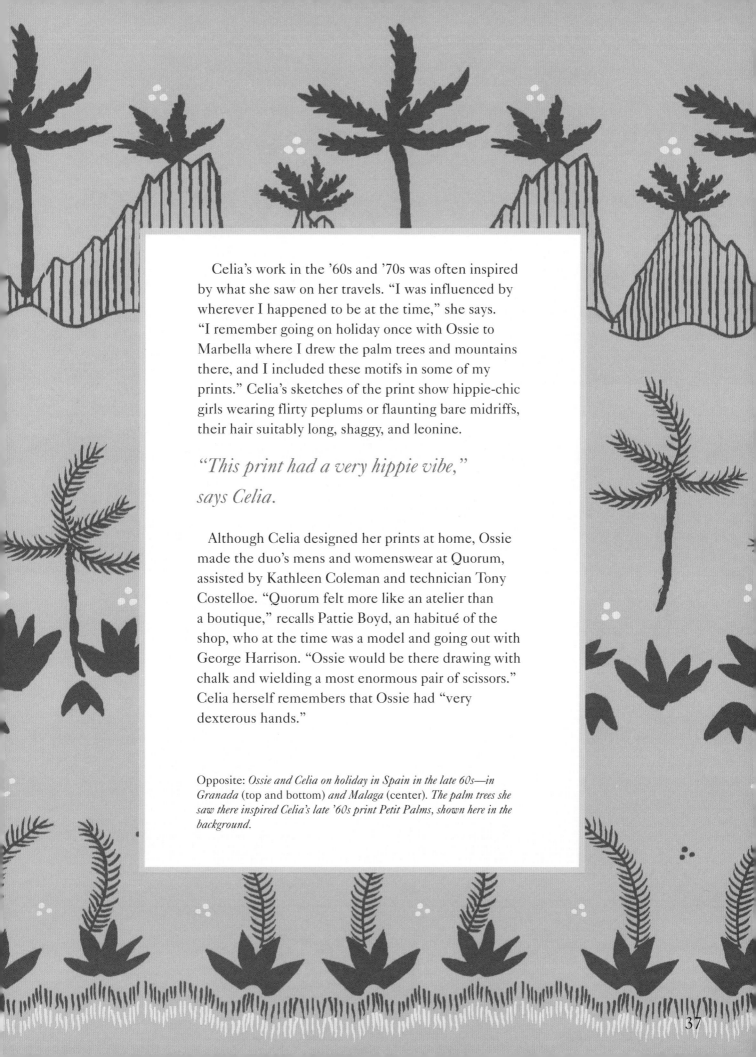

Celia's work in the '60s and '70s was often inspired by what she saw on her travels. "I was influenced by wherever I happened to be at the time," she says. "I remember going on holiday once with Ossie to Marbella where I drew the palm trees and mountains there, and I included these motifs in some of my prints." Celia's sketches of the print show hippie-chic girls wearing flirty peplums or flaunting bare midriffs, their hair suitably long, shaggy, and leonine.

"This print had a very hippie vibe,"
says Celia.

Although Celia designed her prints at home, Ossie made the duo's mens and womenswear at Quorum, assisted by Kathleen Coleman and technician Tony Costelloe. "Quorum felt more like an atelier than a boutique," recalls Pattie Boyd, an habitué of the shop, who at the time was a model and going out with George Harrison. "Ossie would be there drawing with chalk and wielding a most enormous pair of scissors." Celia herself remembers that Ossie had "very dexterous hands."

Opposite: *Ossie and Celia on holiday in Spain in the late 60s—in Granada* (top and bottom) *and Malaga* (center). *The palm trees she saw there inspired Celia's late '60s print Petit Palms, shown here in the background.*

Above: *Model Suki Poitier and Ossie at Quorum, on Radnor Walk, London, circa 1967. Poitier sports a dress made of fabric printed with one of Celia's most iconic prints, Mystic Daisy (the print shown here in the background). Quorum's sample machinist Kathleen Coleman stands to the right of Ossie.*

By 1968, Quorum, whose walls were pasted with marbled paper, and the King's Road had become a mecca for the ultra-hip. Trendy unisex model agency English Boy occupied the floor above, and fashionable restaurant The Casserole, whose clientele included David Bailey and Rudolph Nureyev, was nearby. David Gilmour, of Pink Floyd, was the shop's van driver. A record player belted out the latest hits by the Isley Brothers, the Beatles, the Stones, and R&B.

"Quorum wasn't on a main drag like Biba," remembers Pattie Boyd. "It was more intimate, and you'd bump into people you knew, or you saw famous actors. Quorum's clothes were more cutting edge and expensive. All those chiffon and slinky crepe clothes were for special occasions." And, crucially, in comparison to the demure, old-world style of Biba, Ossie and Celia's creations were sexy. In her book *In Vogue—Six Decades of Fashion*, Georgina Howell described them as "hothouse dresses." "Ossie Clark's satin dresses with fabric prints by Celia Birtwell make the most revealing evening dresses in London,

"Quorum felt more like an atelier than a boutique."

slashed or flowing against the body to show every
line." Not that Ossie and Celia confined themselves to
diaphanous chiffon or clingy crepe and satin dresses.
In 1968, they created the popular Lamborghini suit—a
long, close-fitting, plain satin jacket worn with trousers
featuring a chinoiserie-inspired Celia print. "Quorum
was different from other boutiques," remembers
Kathleen Coleman. "They used very expensive
materials. People sometimes saved up a whole
month's wages to buy clothes there." To begin with,
Quorum sold only couture, although in 1968 clothing
manufacturer Alfred Radley bought the boutique and
introduced a more affordable diffusion line, employing
the designer Rosie Bradford to adapt Ossie's dresses
for a wider market.

Celia and Ossie were now the darlings of the era's
jet set and rock aristocracy. In 1967, Ossie, always a
fervent diary keeper, recorded that the Rolling Stones'
Brian Jones, who lived near Quorum at 52 Radnor
Walk, and Keith Richards were both wearing "silks
and satins printed by Celia."

OSSIE CLARK
MADE IN LONDON, ENGLAND
DRY CLEAN ONLY 12
PRINT BY Celia Birtwell
Quorum RECOMMEND
DRY CLEANING & VALETING
8-10 Pont Street SW1 Tel:235110

40 *Celia Birtwell*

This page: *Celia's early '70s print Baroque Bouquet.*
Opposite: *Bianca Jagger wearing an Indian Bouquet dress, with husband Mick at a party soon after they got married in 1971.*

41

Left: *Celia and Ossie photographed by* Vogue, *July 1970.*
Opposite: *Model and actress Marisa Berenson wearing a dress with Celia's print Baroque Bouquet.*

"Ossie Clark's satin dresses with fabric prints by Celia Birtwell make the most revealing evening dresses in London, slashed or flowing against the body to show every line."

Jimi Hendrix, Talitha Getty, Paloma Picasso, Marisa Berenson, Mick and Bianca Jagger, and Marianne Faithfull also swooned over the duo's glamorous confections. Ossie designed the chiffon and silk velvet dress Bianca wore on the evening of her wedding day in Saint Tropez in 1971. By then, Quorum had moved to new premises on the King's Road. Its name spelled out in neon, the two-story boutique had smoked glass windows and, inside, fake-wood-paneled walls and a black rubber floor. Clothes ranged from the cheaper "Ossie Clark for Radley" ready-to-wear range (under

£20 a garment) to couture pieces priced around £300. Such was the popularity of Celia and Ossie's clothes in the early '70s that shoplifting there was rife.

In 1970, in a further coup for the couple, Ossie was invited by the high-end French manufacturer Mendes, which produced Yves Saint Laurent's Rive Gauche lines and ready-to-wear for Courrèges and Givenchy, to create a collection. Presented in Paris in April 1971, it was well received. But wayward as ever, Ossie missed several business appointments set up by Mendes, and the collaboration fizzled out after the one collection.

ballets russes

An early Celia print featured vibrant yellow and green concentric circles, which Ossie fashioned into a dress with godets (triangular pieces of fabric inserted in the skirt to make it fuller) and Western-style fringing, nodded to Bakst's Ballets Russes costumes for Nijinksy. The dancer was a hero to both Celia and Ossie, who gave their son George the same middle name. In its October 1, 1969, issue, British *Vogue* described its main fashion shoot thus: "Free adaptations from the classics—Diaghilev and Paris salons." In one fashion sketch around this time, Celia paired this Ballets Russes inspired print with a very early appearance of the splashy, large-scale Candyflower—a flower enclosing a swirly motif—one of her most iconic designs, which she has revisted in recent years.

Left: A photograph by Jim Lee showing a dress with Celia's print nodding to Bakst's Ballets Russes costumes for Nijinksy. Ossie added Western-style fringing.
Right: A sketch showing the same print combined with a very early appearance of Celia's swirly late '60s print Candyflower (shown blown up next to the sketch), another of her iconic designs.

Celia's prints were just as appealing as Ossie's famous "architectural" cutting. Philip Prowse believes that Celia's designs are enriched by a sophisticated knowledge of fine art—the result of "having started at art school from a very early, impressionable age, and picking up on things most people normally don't. She's a clever colorist and I think inspired by art; her designs have a light French quality—the loose, free drawing and painting of Dufy and Bonnard." Celia acknowledges the influence of Paul Poiret, partly because she can relate to his interest in the crossover between fine art and the applied arts, and cites a key quote of Poiret's taken from her monograph on him: "Am I a fool when I dream of putting art into my dresses, a fool when I say dressmaking is art? For I have always loved painters, and felt on an equal footing with them. It seems to me that we practise the same craft."

Another aspect of Celia's prints is their mixing of different scales and proportions, as well as the dynamic blend of different prints. "I liked combining a family of prints on the same dress," she says, "For example a quite elaborate one with a simple check." Says Linda Watson:

"Celia's prints brought Ossie's designs to life. The clever way the patterns combined different scales drew the eye from one part of the dress to another."

"There's a randomness about them yet a precise attention to detail." "Celia's very good at juxtaposing different prints," says Vanessa Denza. "Most textile designers aren't." This randomness reflects Celia's interest in the baroque. "I like its fascination with irregularity: with asymmetry in nature, like the idea of the unformed pearl. I like the neo-baroque style of artist Rex Whistler, and designers Oliver Messel, Emilio Terry and Christian Bérard."

Opposite: *A fashion sketch demonstrating Celia's flair for creating a patchwork of prints—a formula she used to balance different designs harmoniously.*

: A voluminous Mystic Daisy
dress photographed by David
gomery for British Vogue,
1969.

Above: *Celia wore the same dress at her very informal
wedding to Ossie in 1969 at Kensington Registry Office;
their only guests were his sister Kay (who wore an Ossie/
Celia moss crepe dress) and David Hockney. At the time,
Celia was pregnant with her first son, Albert.*

"It gives a strong message of the mood of the late '60s and early '70s—it's evocative of Flower Power and psychedelia—yet it's had a very long life."

Another print to emerge in the late '60s was Mystic Daisy, one of Celia's most iconic fashion prints. A shirt with this print was worn in the movie *Cabaret* by Liza Minnelli, all of whose costumes were provided by Quorum. "I designed the print in half an hour at home. The moment I'd done it, I knew it was good. It's got a great sense of rhythm. It's the perfect doodle," remembers Celia, who wore a voluminous Mystic Daisy-print dress when she got married to Ossie at Kensington Registry Office in London in August 1969. The wedding was an extremely intimate, informal, thoroughly modern affair, to which they invited only Hockney and Ossie's sister Kay. Celia was pregnant at the time with Albert, and her father had written to persuade her to get married. The day after, in an eccentric move that presaged the unconventional nature of their marriage, Ossie took off on honeymoon to Barbados—solo.

The joyful, ultradecorative Mystic Daisy, which Celia later used for a furnishing fabric, was a runaway hit. "It gives a strong message of the mood of the late '60s and early '70s—it's evocative of Flower Power and psychedelia—yet it's had a very long life," says Celia. Proof of its longevity came in 2006, when Celia, having tweaked it slightly, used it in her sellout collection for Topshop, the womenswear chain. "It works better as a dress than as a furnishing fabric," she opines.

"It needs to be seen in movement on the girl wearing it."

Opposite: *Actress Jane Birkin photographed by Patrick Lichfield in a top mixing the prints Mystic Daisy and Check and in trousers with the print Lollipop.*

Right: *Ali McGraw modeling an Ossie dress with Celia prints.*
Left: *A jersey dress made of Celia's prints Candyflower and Check, photographed by David Montgomery for British Vogue in 1969.*

"Celia's very good at juxtaposing different prints; most textile designers aren't."

Another key print was Monkey Puzzle. "Its clover leaf and clumps of grass motifs were inspired by medieval English tapestries I'd seen at the V&A," says Celia. It was made of chiffon and cut by Ossie in his inimitable way. It had a medieval feel to it, and to make it fuller, he gave the skirt lots of godets with hems that tapered into handkerchief points. "It had lots of pearl buttons down the front," remembers Celia. "And a tight bodice—Ossie liked those. They pulled bosoms in and made plump women look alluring. That was Ossie's genius."

The '20s and Cubism influence continued with Jazz Flower and the surreally titled Plastic Buildings. Two freer prints, with voluptuous flowers, were Golden Slumbers and Peachy Pie, which Celia and Ossie sometimes combined with the smaller-scale Michaelmas Daisy. Celia liked small prints as much as large and splashy ones; she also created the two prints Lily of the Valley and Pineapple. "These were influenced by '30s day dresses," says Celia. "I like ladylike, small prints, ones worn by women of a certain age." In July 1969, Celia photographed model Gala Mitchell in a dress combining Golden Slumbers and Michaelmas Daisy in the lush Kingston garden of Sheila Oldham, former wife of Andrew Loog Oldham, the Rolling Stones' manager. In the Art Nouveau retro spirit of the time, the garden boasted a rock garden, gigantic ferns, and peacock chairs.

"Her designs have a light French quality—the loose, free drawing and painting of Dufy and Bonnard," says Philip Prowse

Celia's clover leaf Monkey Puzzle print was inspired by medieval tapestries which she'd seen at the V&A. Ossie cut the fabric into a dress with medieval-looking bell sleeves. It was photographed in Ethiopia (opposite) *by Norman Parkinson for British* Vogue, *January 1969, and also photographed* (overleaf) *by Jim Lee.*

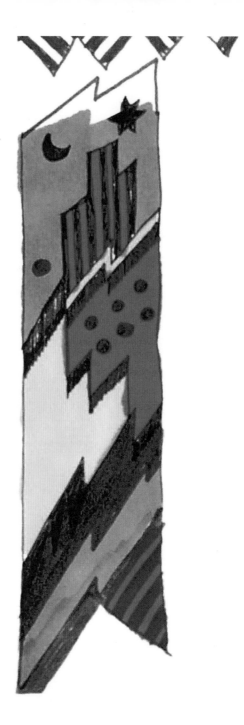

Celia's late '60s sketches featuring her Cubist-inspired, geometric Plastic Buildings and Cubist prints (the earliest examples of which were commissioned by Alice Pollock, the original owner of Quorum and (far right) Flower Ink Spots.

58 *Celia Birtwell*

Left, right, and overleaf: *More Cubist-inspired prints from Celia's Plastic Buildings period, including Gypsy Rose (left). The latter was available as a scarf sold at Quorum (above).*

Celia's lovely photographs of model Gala Mitchell in 1969 in a dress combining her prints Golden Slumbers and Michaelmas Daisy. Gala was posing in the Kingston garden of Sheila Oldham, former wife of Andrew Loog Oldham, the Rolling Stones' manager.

Model and actress Ingrid Boulting photographed by Norman Parkinson for British Vogue, *July, 1970, in a dress featuring a mix of large and small Michaelmas Daisy and Jazz Flower prints (left),* and *in a Golden Slumbers and Michaelmas Daisy print dress (right). The venue was Lacock Abbey, former home of the photography pioneer William Fox Talbot, which inspired the 'old photograph' look of the shoot.*

The two fashion prints (opposite) *incorporate the beginnings of Celia's Michaelmas Daisy prints. The one on this page features an early version of her heraldic, fleur-de-lys-inspired print Little Rock.*

Far left: *A sketch featuring Celia's print Tartan Tulips mixed with Lantern Checks, an early version of her Tulips print.*
Left and above: *Actress Jane Birkin wearing* (left) *a dress with a chiffon top half featuring Celia's Check print and a bottom half in worsted crepe, and* (right) *a jersey dress in Michaelmas Daisy print with a top panel in Jazz Flower print.*
Background: *Michaelmas Daisy.*

Left: *A sketch showing Celia's print Peachy Pie designed to be made out of flannel muslin, on a background of Peachy Pie fabric made of silk twill.*
Above: *A cotton jersey dress mixing Peachy Pie with a different, larger version of Michaelmas Daisy, photographed by Patrick Lichfield for* American Vogue, *1970.*

73

74 Celia Birtwell

Quorum was particularly popular with a new in-crowd now gravitating to the King's Road. One of its ringleaders was Christopher Gibbs, an antique dealer, aesthete, and socialite who was instrumental in bringing together the like-minded bohemian stars of two generations who were kindred spirits for both being rebellious and dressing dandyishly. On the one hand Cecil Beaton and Lady Diana Cooper; on the other were Mick Jagger, Keith Richards, Ossie, Celia, and Hockney. Says Celia:

"This was all part of London in the Swinging Sixties when people of different classes were mixing much more."

"Beaton was curious about the younger generation and he could connect with them, with their bohemian taste, regardless of their background."

Celia met Beaton in 1971, visiting him at his home, Reddish House, in Wiltshire, with Ossie and Hockney. "I remember we were a bit late and he wasn't too happy," remembers Celia. 'His house was exquisite; some of the walls were covered in navy blue velvet, and there were the palest pastel pink roses on a table and stripped oak floors painted ivory with rugs on them. We sat in the conservatory, which had a black and white checkerboard floor, lots of auriculas in different colors, lots of wicker furniture, and the sound of water from a little fountain. Beaton was wearing a dark green velvet suit—very chic."

Left: *Celia, Ossie (holding Albert), and Hockney on their way to visit Cecil Beaton at his home, Reddish House, in Wiltshire, in 1971. Celia wore an Ossie viscose crepe-de-chine dress with a rickrack-trimmed suede bib made using her print Black-eyed Susan.*
Below: *Celia and Ossie's sons Albert (left) and George snapped at Hockney's home in Powis Terrace, London by Mo McDermott.*

Background: *Black-eyed Susan print—one of her discharge designs printed on a black background.*

Overleaf, clockwise from left: *Celia's design Lily Marlene —inspired by her love of lilies and later renamed Little Rock —printed on a velvet dress, photographed by Clive Arrowsmith for British* Vogue; *Celia at her home in Linden Gardens; Mo McDermott, wearing a shirt with a Celia print in front of his iconic cutout trees; model Gala Mitchell photographed at Linden Gardens in a chiffon, Lily Marlene print frock.*
Background: *Celia's print Pineapple.*

A classic Celia print from this period (and one she has used again in recent years) was Lily Marlene, which was printed on velvet and georgette and later renamed Little Rock. "I wanted to do a print with lilies because I've always loved their shape and perfume," says Celia, who photographed model Gala Mitchell at Linden Gardens in a '40s-inspired, halter-neck, chiffon dress with this print, sprawling vampishly in a pose that anticipated Roxy Music's early '70s album covers.

One very effective printing technique Celia particularly liked was discharge printing. "You use a black fabric and bleach out the areas where the motifs are to be printed on first so that when the colors are printed on these parts they really sing against the black," explains Celia, who often wore dresses with her discharge prints, one of which was called Black-eyed Susan. Sometimes Celia's prints were embroidered to similarly dramatic effect onto black fabrics (by a company called Hewitsons in Macclesfield, Cheshire). These were usually cut into tight, ankle-skimming dresses. One bias-cut version was called the Daisy Whirligig dress.

Top left: *A photo of Celia taken by Cecil Beaton in the conservatory of his home, Reddish House, when she visited him in 1971.*
Above right: *Models-of-the-moment Gala Mitchell, Kelly, and Kari-Ann Muller in Ossie's '30s-inspired bias-cut dresses made from Celia's embroidered or discharge floral fabrics, which she created around the same time. They were modeled at Celia and Ossie's Royal Court Theatre catwalk show in 1971.*
Background: *A detail of the same discharge print on the dress Kari-Ann wore at the Royal Court show.*

80   *Celia Birtwell*

At this time, Ossie and Celia were going from strength to strength. Cementing their reputation as the fashion dream team of the late '60s and early '70s were their groundbreaking London catwalk shows, which fused thunderous rock music with models dancing deliriously down the runway—a far cry from the poker-faced mannequins and mostly prissy catwalk shows of the '50s and '60s. Unusually for the time, some of the models were black; and the models were personalities in their own right— charismatic, vampish, and self-consciously decadent: Amanda Lear, Gala Mitchell, Kari-Ann Muller (cover girl of Roxy Music's eponymous 1972 debut album). . . Yet, says Philip Prowse, "People could aspire to look like the models in Celia and Ossie's shows, whereas in the '50s people could never look like them. The clothes were for real people. Instead of that very formal, chiseled impeccable look which '50s models had, now—in the late '60s and early '70s—everyone could have a go. Because Ossie's clothes were cut on the bias, they look good on big girls, not just very skinny ones."

These legendary happenings— at which the models strutted around louchely, high on marijuana and champagne, their giddy abandon emphasizing the sexiness and freedom embodied by Celia and Ossie's provocatively diaphanous frocks — were often compared to pop concerts. They were held at London's Revolution club, where Hendrix and the Rolling Stones were in the audience, in Chelsea Town Hall, in Aretusa, a club on the King's Road, and in the Royal Court Theatre on Sloane Square.

Inset pictures: *Stills of footage of the Royal Court show in 1971 from* A Bigger Splash. *Hockney looks on as models, sporting Celia's discharge and embroidered prints, strut their stuff. And a joyously colorful Celia fashion sketch from the same period.*
Backgrounds: *Celia's candy-motif discharge print* (left) *and embroidered fabric inspired by Elizabethan embroidery* (this page).

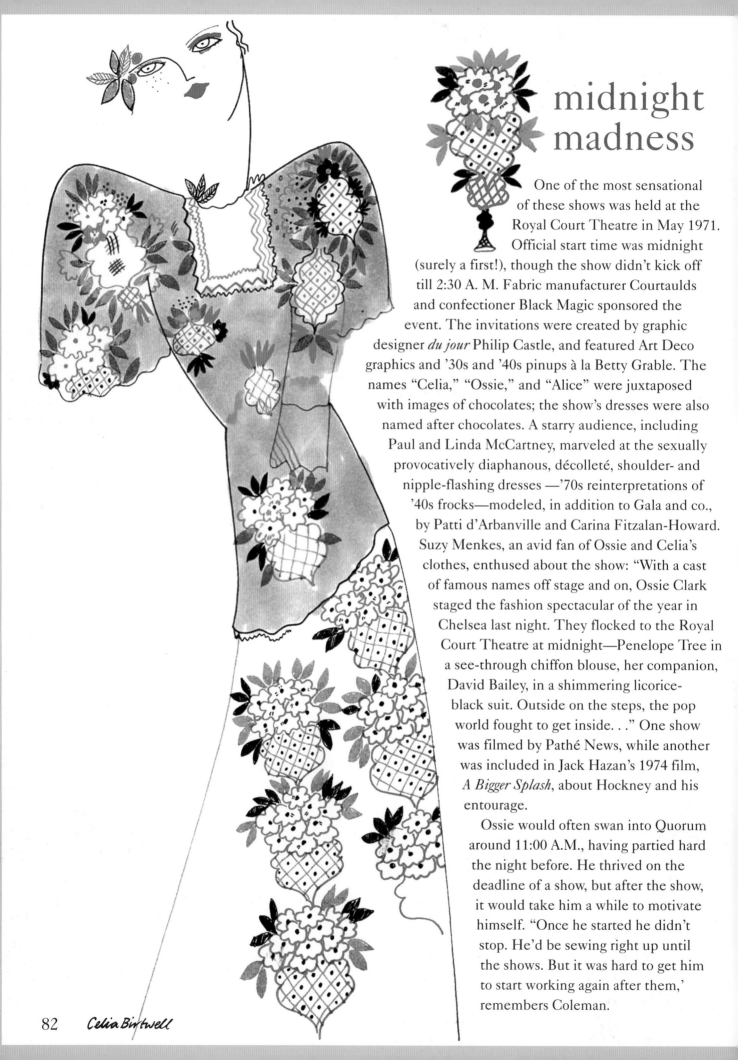

midnight madness

One of the most sensational of these shows was held at the Royal Court Theatre in May 1971. Official start time was midnight (surely a first!), though the show didn't kick off till 2:30 A. M. Fabric manufacturer Courtaulds and confectioner Black Magic sponsored the event. The invitations were created by graphic designer *du jour* Philip Castle, and featured Art Deco graphics and '30s and '40s pinups à la Betty Grable. The names "Celia," "Ossie," and "Alice" were juxtaposed with images of chocolates; the show's dresses were also named after chocolates. A starry audience, including Paul and Linda McCartney, marveled at the sexually provocatively diaphanous, décolleté, shoulder- and nipple-flashing dresses —'70s reinterpretations of '40s frocks—modeled, in addition to Gala and co., by Patti d'Arbanville and Carina Fitzalan-Howard. Suzy Menkes, an avid fan of Ossie and Celia's clothes, enthused about the show: "With a cast of famous names off stage and on, Ossie Clark staged the fashion spectacular of the year in Chelsea last night. They flocked to the Royal Court Theatre at midnight—Penelope Tree in a see-through chiffon blouse, her companion, David Bailey, in a shimmering licorice-black suit. Outside on the steps, the pop world fought to get inside. . ." One show was filmed by Pathé News, while another was included in Jack Hazan's 1974 film, *A Bigger Splash*, about Hockney and his entourage.

Ossie would often swan into Quorum around 11:00 A.M., having partied hard the night before. He thrived on the deadline of a show, but after the show, it would take him a while to motivate himself. "Once he started he didn't stop. He'd be sewing right up until the shows. But it was hard to get him to start working again after them,' remembers Coleman.

Celia Birtwell

Opposite: *The print on this dress, called Gioconda, was part of Celia's family of "bouquet-based" designs with delicate, often small motifs in reds, blues, and greens on white, inspired by her love of gardens. Created around 1972, these defined sharply from the graphic contrasts of her discharge prints.*
Above: *Ossie and Celia at work in his atelier at Quorum with fabrics printed with another of her bouquet-based designs, Tartan Hearts.*

Celia. Nov 10th 1972
GH.

Left: *A portrait of Celia by David Hockney in crayon on paper, 1972. Her dress is made of a chiffon fabric featuring one of her bouquet-based prints (also shown here in the background).*
Below: *An invitation designed by Hockney for an Ossie/Celia fashion show hosted at the Chelsea home of regular Quorum customer and socialite Nicky Waymouth. The address 28 Mallord Street had once been the studio of artist Augustus John.*

Ossie Clark & Celia Birtwell

invite you to see their new

collection for

Quorum

at 28 Mallord St SW3

R.S.V.P. for Entrance tickets
Adrianne Hunter
~~Quorum~~
~~52 Radnor Walk S.W.3~~
tele 352 1083

Compact, delicate motifs in reds, blues, and greens on white, inspired by her love of gardens.

Opposite: *A sketch showing Tartan Hearts. The left-hand sleeve features another bouquet-based print, Vita Flowers and Feathers, named after Vita Sackville-West and her garden at Sissinghurst, in Kent.* Cutouts: *These mini iced cakes, made by London bakery Konditor and Cook, feature motifs— provided by Celia and pictured in a row, below—taken from these prints. The cakes were sold at all the bakery's branches for one month to raise money for charity.* Right: *A georgette dress and quilted silk jacket printed with another bouquet-based design, Marie Antoinette, featured in British* Vogue, *April, 1973*

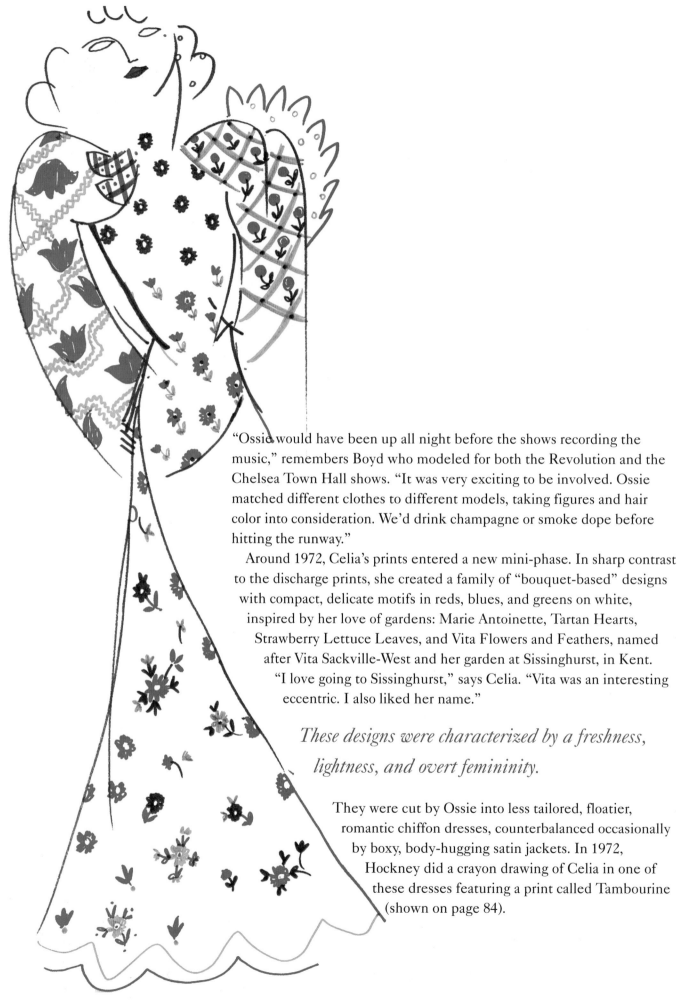

"Ossie would have been up all night before the shows recording the music," remembers Boyd who modeled for both the Revolution and the Chelsea Town Hall shows. "It was very exciting to be involved. Ossie matched different clothes to different models, taking figures and hair color into consideration. We'd drink champagne or smoke dope before hitting the runway."

Around 1972, Celia's prints entered a new mini-phase. In sharp contrast to the discharge prints, she created a family of "bouquet-based" designs with compact, delicate motifs in reds, blues, and greens on white, inspired by her love of gardens: Marie Antoinette, Tartan Hearts, Strawberry Lettuce Leaves, and Vita Flowers and Feathers, named after Vita Sackville-West and her garden at Sissinghurst, in Kent.

"I love going to Sissinghurst," says Celia. "Vita was an interesting eccentric. I also liked her name."

These designs were characterized by a freshness, lightness, and overt femininity.

They were cut by Ossie into less tailored, floatier, romantic chiffon dresses, counterbalanced occasionally by boxy, body-hugging satin jackets. In 1972, Hockney did a crayon drawing of Celia in one of these dresses featuring a print called Tambourine (shown on page 84).

Opposite and right: *Two Celia
sketches showing designs intended
for embroidery.*

"Celia went through a phase of ramping up her palette, creating several riotously, confidently colorful prints."

In 1972, Celia began using more colors than usual for prints, including the semiabstract Delaware, now known as Cha Cha Cha, shown in a sketch by Celia (left). The design on fabric is seen in close-up (right).

Celia Birtwell

bohemian chic

In 1972, Celia went through a phase of ramping up her palette, creating several riotously, confidently colorful prints, including the semiabstract Delaware, now known as Cha Cha Cha (bold florals and calligraphic squiggles); Pretty Woman, named after Roy Orbison's song and featuring anemones and other flowers; Queen of the Night; and the very free, painterly Tulips. Although bold, these designs were often printed on filmy, fairy-wing-light chiffons. The Tulips print was a favorite of a regular Quorum customer, the heiress Nicky Waymouth (married then to Nigel Waymouth, owner of the cult King's Road boutique Granny Takes a Trip), who mixed with the same arty Notting Hill set as did Celia.

Waymouth once hosted a Celia/Ossie show at her sumptuously bohemian house in the artist Augustus John's old studio on 28 Mallord Street, Chelsea. Hockney designed the invitation with a faux-naif, multicolored script. Shooting for British *Vogue*, Norman Parkinson snapped Waymouth in an ankle-skimming Tulips print dress, sprawling in a suitably decadent, supine fashion; strewn nearby was cult book of the day Kenneth Anger's *Hollywood Babylon*, which unearthed the scandals of Hollywood stars. Bianca Jagger modeled, too, along with Pattie, Kari-Ann, and Gala. Waymouth also bought another classic Ossie/Celia design: a black and scarlet, gypsy-chic dress with a star and moon print of 1971.

The gorgeously decorative patterns of these fabrics and prints were even more stunning in movement.

Their photogenic nature ensured that they got plenty of press coverage. Top '70s photographer Barry Lategan, who snapped a model wearing a billowing dress made of the radiantly colorful Delaware print for British *Vogue* in 1972, has commented: "It was very helpful shooting chiffons because one could blow the clothes with a machine. Up until then, pictures had been static." His comment echoes Celia's belief that many of her prints work better when seen on a body in movement.

This page: *A detail of the print Delaware (as it was known in the '70s).*
Right: *A Delaware print dress, photographed by Barry Lategan.*

70s reinterpretations
of 40s frocks . . .
prints with
bold florals and
calligraphic
squiggles.

Left: *Another print,* Pretty Woman, *part of the same series of colorful designs as* Delaware, *and named after Roy Orbison's song, features anemones and other flowers.*
Right: *A variation of the same print.*

Although bold,
these designs were
often printed on
filmy, fairy-wing-
light chiffons.

Left and right: Tulips, *another exuberantly
vibrant design from this period.*

98   Celia Birtwell

Tulips *seen in close-up* (left) *and on a dress worn by Nicky Waymouth* (above).

Overleaf: *Nicky Waymouth wearing the* Tulips *print dress in her sumptuously bohemian house on Mallord Street, London. Waymouth was photographed by Norman Parkinson for British* Vogue, *December, 1972.*

Celia Birtwell

Above: *Celia at work, photographed by Peter Schlesinger; she is wearing an Ossie jacket with embroidered cuffs, which she loved.*
Background: *Celia's print Pretty Woman in a softer colorway.*

the end of a golden era

While Celia and Ossie were the toast of London at the time, Quorum's fortunes began to slide. Quorum had a successful wholesale side (selling in Germany, Italy, Switzerland, and the U. S.); 20,000 copies of a Mystic Daisy print dress were sold, for example. But business was badly affected by the fact that other stores were selling cheap copies of their clothes and that Quorum didn't have enough variety of stock to lure the public.

At this point, Celia was working with Courtaulds and designing woven and embroidered as well as printed fabrics. Meanwhile, relations between Al Radley and Ossie—whose partnership with Pollock was rumoured to have ended—were deteriorating. For Ossie, Quorum was becoming increasingly commercial, and he felt his artistic freedom had become compromised. His star was also falling, perhaps because he was competing for media attention with other British designers now appearing on the scene, such as Bill Gibb and Antony Price.

Ossie would also soon be out of sync with the direction fashion was heading in the mid-'70s. Fast eclipsing the romanticism of the early '70s was contemporary minimalist, workwear-influenced clothing, on the one hand, and the beginnings of punk style on the other. "The press went off Ossie," suggests Linda Watson. This, and the breakup with Celia soon after, marked the start of Ossie's decline. (He pleaded bankruptcy in the late '70s, and his career continued to deteriorate; sadly he died in 1996.)

Two Celia prints designed circa 1973; the left-hand one is called Babylon (also seen in close-up in the background).

Overleaf: *Celia photographed at Linden Gardens by Peter Schlesinger in the early '70s* (left). Background: *Monkey Puzzle print.*

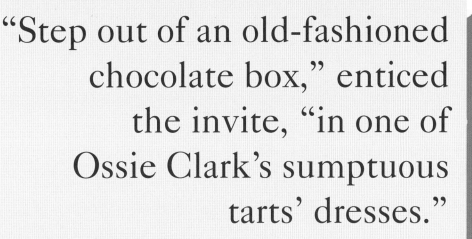

"Step out of an old-fashioned chocolate box," enticed the invite, "in one of Ossie Clark's sumptuous tarts' dresses."

But back in 1973, the two were still designing together. In April that year, Quorum showed a collection reflecting the increasingly fashionable trend for '50s retro already being pushed by designers such as Price and Vivienne Westwood. The invitation to the show (which once again was sponsored by Black Magic) pictured a man in a '50s-inspired suit and a trilby and a Rosalind Russell-style vamp in an off-the-shoulder Ossie dress with Celia-print sleeves. "Step out of an old-fashioned chocolate box," it enticed, "in one of Ossie Clark's sumptuous tarts' dresses."

In July, Celia and Ossie's autumn/winter collection was unveiled at Aretusa, attended by Bianca Jagger. Most of the models were black, and the clothes were made of classic Celia prints, with her checkerboard patterns and Pineapple motif resurfacing. Ossie played with different shapes: a detachable wrap skirt was worn over a romper-style suit with a deep decolleté. In terms of Celia and Ossie's collaboration, the show was very much their last hurrah.

Their personal lives were increasingly stormy. Celia and Ossie, who was less and less in control of his drug-taking, separated in 1973; they divorced the following year. But they continued to work together briefly. Their autumn/winter 1974 collection was staged at the King's Road Theatre, where the newish Rocky Horror Show was playing. Hockney, Marianne Faithfull, Bryan Ferry, Britt Ekland, and Ringo Starr attended. The clothes, made using Celia prints and incorporating tightly boned, Victorian-style bustiers, were more fitted and structured than usual.

Beauty and the father in house
caroomes July 1970
J Purdy [?]

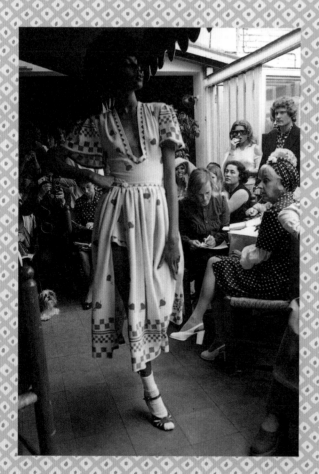

Opposite, top: *A watercolor portrait by Patrick Procktor of Ossie and Celia called "Beauty and the Beast," 1969.*
Opposite, center: *Carina Fitzalan-Howard, who often modeled for Ossie and Celia, seen with him in one of his and Celia's confections.*
Opposite, bottom: *Celia and Ossie's last fashion show at hip restaurant and nightclub Aretusa, on London's King's Road. In the audience were two Quorum employees—technician Tony Costelloe, standing to the right, and Alice Pollock's sample machinist, Isabel Gavabitas, with dark hair, seated.*
Background: *Celia's graphic, semiabstract Eye print, created circa 1975, to be printed on crepe-de-chine. Celia was influenced at the time by the drawings of Jean Cocteau and the paintings of Fernand Léger.*
Below: *Novelist and Ritz magazine's gossip columnist Frances Lynn, wearing a Celia silk blouse with the same print, seen with fellow gossip columnist Nigel Dempster.*

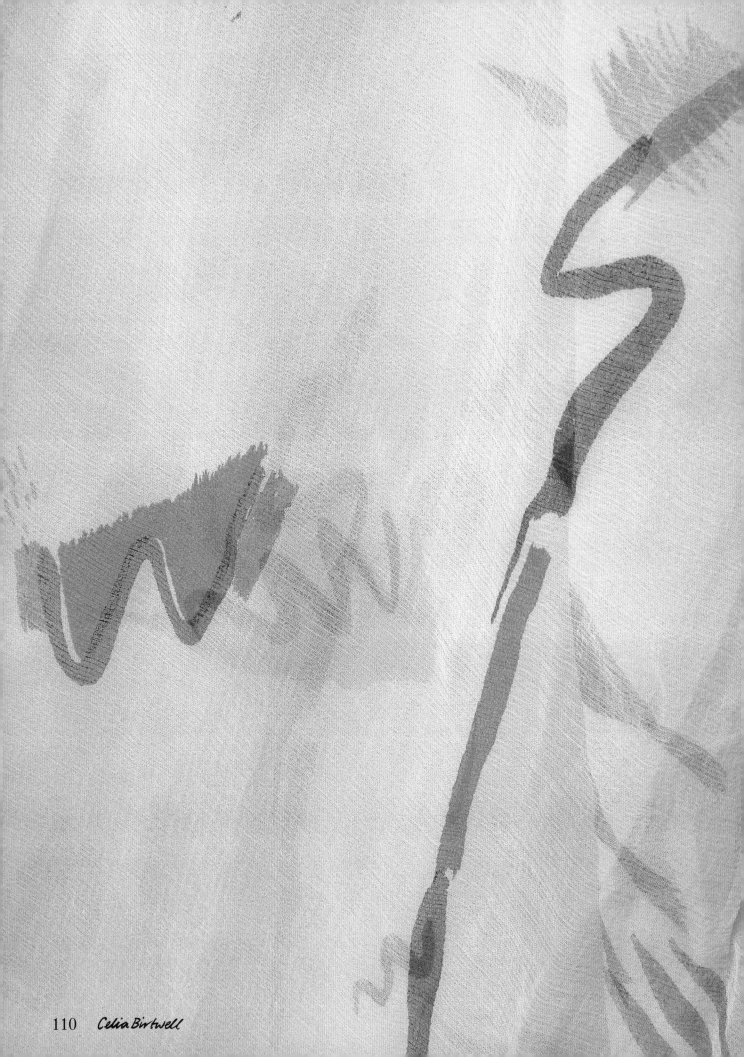

110   *Celia Birtwell*

*In the mid-'70s Celia's designs were inspired by the pointillist painter Georges Seurat. They were abstract and featured calligraphic squiggles and dashes—as shown by these sketches (*right*) and an actual fabric (*left, seen in close-up*) from this period. A model photographed at Leighton House, London (*above*), wears a dress with the print illustrated here.*

Celia's designs became more abstract and graphic . . . they reflected fashion's move away from romanticism and floral patterns.

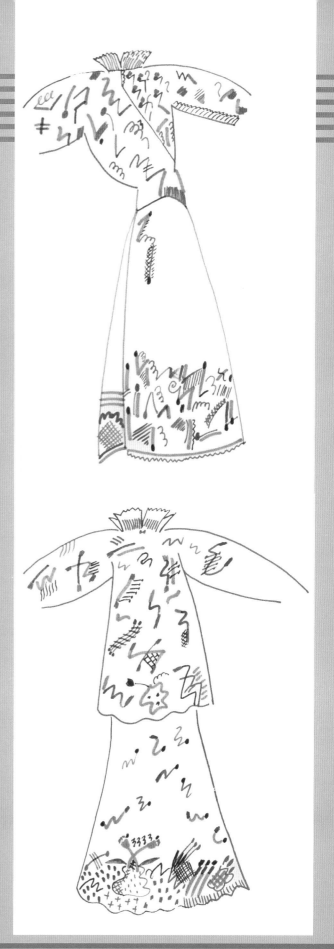

Celia was also inspired by artists Jean Cocteau and Fernand Léger as well as Georges Seurat.

More fashion sketches (left and below)—*and a detail of fabric* (opposite)—*once again show the influence of pointillism on Celia.*

From the mid-'70s, Celia went out with the artist Adrian George for about four years. She was still designing prints for Radley, creating two fabric collections a year in a studio on Eastcastle Street, near Oxford Circus. But in 1976 her working relationship with Radley came to an end. Around this time, her designs became more abstract and graphic, and a major influence on her was the pointillist painter Georges Seurat. She also created her Forest, Eye, and Scratch prints, which, calligraphic and semiabstract, reflected fashion's move away from romanticism and floral patterns. Celia's new designs incorporated '50s elements like peplums and black lace, which she describes as "cowboyish." But the influences for these prints were more wide-ranging: she was also inspired by artists Jean Cocteau and Fernand Léger.

Soon after, Celia left the fashion industry to raise her sons and teach at art colleges across London. And she worked as a paid model for David Hockney.

topshop

Celia's career in fashion enjoyed a spectacular renaissance in 2006 with her sellout capsule collection for Topshop. Vanessa Denza put forward Celia's name to Jane Shepherdson, then Topshop's brand director, with a view to a collaboration. Shepherdson was very enthusiastic about this and introduced her to head buyer Caren Downie. The collaboration was a huge success. "The buyers knew exactly what they wanted and if I didn't like something I could say so, and they listened," remembers Celia. Reviving such archive prints as Mystic Daisy, she created a sexy, swirly, flattering line of dresses and blouses in her trademark fabrics—silk, georgette and voile.

In fact, Topshop's instinctive understanding that her timeless, must-have prints would appeal to noughties fashionistas proved spot-on. The runaway success of her inexpensive designs—launched in April 2006—is now the stuff of legend; the special-edition collection, stocked by Topshop's Oxford Street flagship store, sold out immediately. This affordable collection of Celia's prints introduced a whole new generation to her work.

Left: *A blouse and dress from Celia's sellout Topshop collection of 2006, and a photo of Kate Moss wearing a dress from it* (bottom, left).
Above: *Celia dresses in the windows of Topshop.*
Top and right: *Celia's fashion sketches for the collection.*

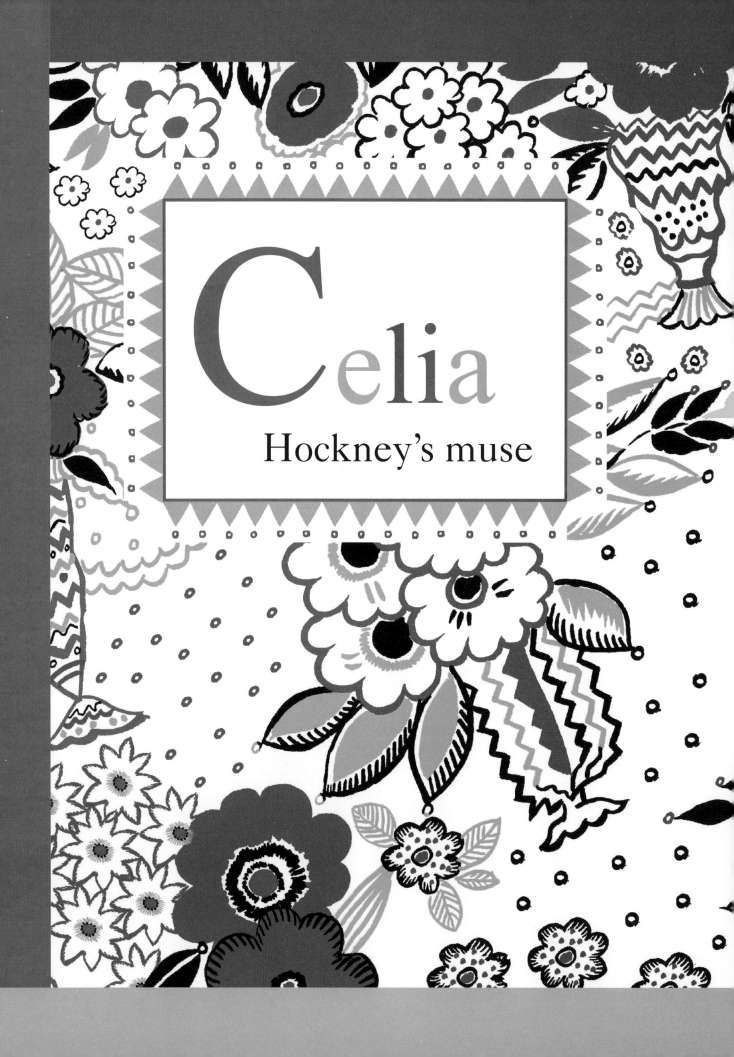

Celia
Hockney's muse

Left: *One of David Hockney's first portraits of Celia, an etching and aquatint of 1969, simply called* Celia. *She is wearing the Mystic Daisy print dress she wore at her wedding.*
Right: *Celia and Hockney at his flat in Powis Terrace, Notting Hill, 1969, photographed by Hockney's former boyfriend Peter Schlesinger.*

sitting on one—and an old-fashioned dressing table."

In the '60s and '70s, before its gentrification, Notting Hill was completely different, remembers Hockney. "Hardly any building was painted, it was all peeling paint, all dark. Nothing had been done to these houses for 20 or 30 years. It was cheap living in them because they were so run-down. I knew students who lived in a big one with a garden near Portobello market. It would now cost three or four million pounds." Notting Hill was vibrantly bohemian. "Chelsea was much more respectable," says Hockney. Celia says, "I went to Chelsea a lot because of Quorum, but never got to know it . . . It was very upper-class even then. Notting Hill was a bit down and out. People would say, 'Oooh, you live in Notting Hill' with a slight shudder."

Kindred spirits Celia and Hockney, however, were in their element: "People earned livings," he says. "But no one had much money. Yet no one complained. They thought life was marvelous, and it was. People, a lot of them art students, were genuinely bohemian, free spirits. There was free sex."

"People there were attracted to other free spirits. Bohemia had characters."

"I think the reason you don't have them now is because people call them losers. Bohemia didn't judge them. It recognized they were frail but had things to give."

"The bohemian world was separate from the world of respectability, which you weren't part of. Celia wasn't keen on her parents coming to London often—and they didn't. She was very fond of them, but they might have been shocked at her lifestyle. In London she was having such a good time, feeling independent. She had no intention of going back to Salford." "My father always used to say to me, 'Have you had enough yet, are you coming home yet?'" interjects Celia.

bohemian rhapsody

Celia first saw Hockney in 1968; Pauline Boty had pointed him out on Portobello Road, wearing a maroon corduroy jacket; but, uncharacteristically, he didn't have his trademark bleached-blond hair. "Pauline said, intriguingly, 'He's quite something. He's a force to be reckoned with,'" Celia remembers. "I later met David through Ossie as they were friends at the R. C. A. Mo, who'd later be David's assistant, was another friend of David's. Mo told me to go to David's R. C. A. degree show, which included his marvelous painting *The Cruel Elephant*, with an elephant trampling over the words 'crawling insects.' It was Mo who first told me about his pictures. Hockney had given him an etching from his *Rake's Progress* series which Mo had on his wall."

Celia sometimes stayed at Hockney's flat in Powis Terrace, Notting Hill, with Ossie, in a room with "a sign saying 'Get Up And Work,'" she recalls. "He had chintz-covered chairs—he made a portrait of Mo

Celia and Hockney also bonded through traveling. He invited Celia to go to Paris with him in the late '60s. It was there that he did his first pen drawing of Celia. "David and I both like France and went to Paris a lot," says Celia. "We'd go to exhibitions, galleries, restaurants. We'd go to the Louvre and smaller galleries on the Rue de Seine. We shared a love of Picasso. David's much more knowledgable about painting. He really studies it. He goes to lots of exhibitions, sometimes to the same one three times."

"She'd come to Paris for three or four days," says Hockney. "I'd draw her a lot, dine out. We saw a big Matisse show at the Grand Palais in 1973. She's a lover of French painting. She's good to go round galleries with, she really looks at pictures, she's got a very good eye."

Celia also hit it off with Hockney's then boyfriend Peter Schlesinger, whom he'd met while teaching at UCLA. "I got on with Peter instantly; he's quite home loving and often came round to see me at home," recalls Celia. "He was painting at the time—and photographing his friends—and had a studio nearby."

There were a variety of other reasons why Celia and Hockney clicked, she says. "We're both from the North. I'm from Lancashire, he's from Yorkshire." "By the mid-'60s, being a provincial Northerner was no longer a disadvantage in Britain," remembers

"She's good to go round galleries with, she really looks at pictures, she's got a very good eye."

Hockney. "The Beatles had a big effect. They were from Liverpool, meaning provincial, but were very confident, proud of where they came from." "David and I had similar family backgrounds," she adds. "We both had strong mothers. Our fathers were both conscientious objectors and rather eccentric. David's father wore three wristwatches, painted patterns on his shirt collars, and stuck stickers of spots on his tie. He'd buy second-hand prams, restore them with David's mother, then sell them by leaving ads for them with his phone number in phone boxes close by! David and I also both like Laurel and Hardy films, like my father did."

In the summer of 1969, Celia, Hockney, and Schlesinger stayed at director Tony Richardson's house in Saint-Tropez. "I was pregnant with Albert," remembers Celia. "The place was gorgeous and high up in the hills. The swimming pool was in David's painting *Portrait of An Artist (Pool with Two Figures)*, of 1971, which he struggled with. The figure in the pink jacket staring into the pool is Peter." In his autobiography *Hockney by Hockney*, the artist wrote: "I drew a lot closer to Celia at that time, and started making more drawings of her."

Above: Celia in Red, *a colored pencil and oil crayon drawing by Hockney, 1970.*
Right: Celia with Hockney in Paris, 1970, *photographed by Schlesinger.*

Above: *Celia in the living room at Linden Gardens* (top), *1970, and in the bedroom where she and Ossie posed for Hockney's iconic, well-loved painting* Mr and Mrs Clark and Percy (bottom). *The bedroom was made to resemble a living room.*

Opposite: *Some of Hockney's photos of Celia posing for the painting.*

Pages 122–125: *Celia on holiday at director Tony Richardson's house, Le Nid du Duc, in the hills above Saint-Tropez in 1969. She went with Hockney, who took most of these pictures, and Schlesinger.*

mr. and mrs. clark

In 1969, the year he was best man at Celia and Ossie's wedding, Hockney began doing preparatory drawings for *Mrs and Mrs Clark and Percy*—the now-iconic painting in which Celia and Ossie pose with hip nonchalance, their arty home suffused with a chalky light and sparsely, fashionably furnished with an Art Nouveau Tiffany lamp, Madonna lilies, shag pile rug and white phone on the floor. This work made it into the final ten of BBC Radio 4's "Greatest Painting in Britain Vote" in 2005, the only work by a living artist to do so.

"I spent a lot of time in Linden Gardens—or Linden Splinge, as Celia called it," Hockney says, explaining its genesis. "Often if Peter and I had been somewhere, we'd go to Linden Gardens before going home: smoke a joint, watch something on TV."

"That room where the painting was done was a nice place to sit."

"I spent about six months on it, doing two or three other paintings, too, but not as big. I'd done a double portrait of two friends in New York, so I thought Celia and Ossie would be a good subject." Indeed, *Mr and Mrs Clark and Percy* was one of a series of double portraits of people very close to Hockney that he had embarked on two years before with a double portrait of art curator Henry Geldzahler and the painter Christopher Scott. Hockney's friends often sit for him because, he says, "a level of intimacy with my subjects is important."

Celia and Ossie, she in an Ossie dress, her hair in Botticelli-esque curls, posed in the bedroom at Linden Gardens. Hockney rearranged the furniture to make it resemble a living room and simplified the décor. One wag later dubbed the painting "Bottichelsea style"— though it was painted in far more hip Notting Hill, this captured the painting's early '70s boho glamour. In fact, Hockney was influenced by the *Arnolfini Portrait* by Jan van Eyck—appropriately, since Celia was pregnant with George—and by William Hogarth's *A Rake's Progress*.

"David decided to paint us in this room because

he liked its proportions. He chose the objects in it to reflect our personalities," Celia remembers. "Originally I was going to pose in a blue djellaba from Marrakesh, but then switched to the Ossie dress."

"David included our cat Blanche, but renamed her Percy as he thought it had a better ring."

Hockney also worked a lot from photographs. "I kept taking photographs, making drawings, trying to work out the composition before I began," he wrote in *Hockney by Hockney*. "Apart from the unfinished picture of George [Lawson] and Wayne [Sleep], this is the painting that comes closest to naturalism … as opposed to realism. The figures are nearly life-size; it's difficult painting figures like that … Ossie was painted many times. I probably painted the head alone 12 times … You can see the paint gets thicker there."

"The one great technical problem is that it's contre-jour; the source of the light is from the middle of the painting, which does create problems . . . It's easier if the source of light is from the side and you can't see it; because if you can see it, it has to be the lightest thing in the painting; and so it creates problems about tone … Although the figures were painted from life a great deal they were posed in my studio because the painting is very big. What I wanted to achieve by such a big painting was the presence of two people in this room. All the technical problems were caused because my main aim was to paint the relationship of these two people. Somebody … commented that most of my double portraits are like Annunciations; there's always somebody who looks permanent and somebody who's a kind of visitor. Here it's odd that Ossie is sitting down . . . but Celia's standing up. That causes a slight disturbance, because you know it should be reversed."

Indeed, the painting can be seen as a sign of the times, reflecting growing gender equality in the '70s.

This makes it opposed to, say, Gainsborough's double portraits, in which husbands stand proprietorially, while their wives sit demurely next to them—literally in an inferior position.

But in an interview for this book, Hockney said that for all this analysis, Celia and Ossie's positions were simply observed from life: "It was more what happened. Celia did stand up more—as you can see, Celia is standing now! Whereas Ossie, given the chance, always sat down. You notice things like that if you're painting people."

Celia and Ossie seem to represent the ideal of a stylish, contemporary couple, but this wasn't Hockney's intention: "How they're depicted is an extension of what they're like," he says. "I was trying do a portrait of two very close friends whom I was spending a lot of time with, not making a social comment. Yes, the setting was stylish, but Celia and Ossie, not the objects, dominate the room. I'm not denying they had pretty things—Celia's choice of things."

And Ossie's mercurial character and habits explain why he was harder to paint, says Hockney now: "Celia gave me more posing time. Because Ossie lived for the night, he wouldn't get up till 4:00 P.M. But if you're a painter you're generally painting during the day because you want the light. Sometimes Ossie would say, 'I'm going out' —he was going to some nightclub at 1:30 A.M.—and I heard Celia say to him one day, 'Now you come straight home after that club.'"

Previous pages: Mr and Mrs Clark and Percy, *acrylic on canvas, 1970–71*

Above: *Hockney painting* Mr and Mrs Clark and Percy *in 1971.*
Opposite: *Celia in front of the huge canvas, whose figures are almost life-size.*

When Celia first saw the finished painting, she loved its use of color: "It's very gentle. But for some time, I felt I couldn't look at it too closely because it's so personal." It was only years later, when she was involved in setting up an exhibition on Ossie in 1999/ 2000 at the Warrington Museum and Art Gallery with Brian Harris, that she took a good look at it, since the gallery borrowed it for three months. "I really familiarized myself with it, and, for the first time, I spotted that the print on Ossie's collar is Mystic Daisy. I know the painting has sold more postcards in the Tate than any other and that it's the gallery's most popular poster."

Yet, says Hockney, he's unable to fathom why the painting is so well loved: "No analysis I can give you can tell you why. But if you mention its title to people they can describe it reasonably well, the image is strong. It comes into your head. No one knows what makes it memorable. It has to be through certain things: a certain simplicity, its composition, but if you tried to do another it might not work. There's no formula for a memorable image, otherwise there'd be a lot more of them. They just come along. It's true in photography, too. If you say a title, for example, Cartier-Bresson's *Picnic on the Banks of the Marne* to many people, a very powerful image comes into their heads, but they themselves wouldn't know why it's memorable. I don't think anyone does."

"Celia and Ossie's positions were simply observed from life. Celia did stand up more."

lifelong friends

"David's amazing," Celia says. "I feel very honored to be his friend. He's loyal to a few people who've been there for him for a long time. He likes me because he thinks I'm a bit ridiculous. He likes my sense of humor, he says I make him laugh, which is flattering."

Which is indeed what Hockney says about Celia when asked to sum up her personality: "She's playful, funny. When I first met her, I was attracted to the fact she could make me laugh, and that's a very big appeal to me. As I got to know her, what I liked was that she had a very nice way of talking. In those days she used the adjective 'little': everything was described as little, and when I pointed out that I liked it, she stopped. But then she thought up others. She'd add the suffix 'arooji' to everything, very unself-consciously—a cigarette became a 'cigarooji', and so on—a nice habit. I realized I shouldn't point them out because Celia didn't notice how often they were used."

> *"As an artist, he liked my face for some reason," continues Celia.*

"The fact that people recognize me from his portraits of me was another feather in my cap. No one can touch him for his skills in portraiture. He's also shown me lots of lovely places when we've traveled together, places he's found and wants to share. We also both have a passion for 40s films—our favorites are *The Gang's All Here* with Carmen Miranda, *Singin' in the Rain*, and *Great Expectations*, with Jean Simmons."

In spring 1970, Celia went with Hockney to New York – her first trip there. 'David was going anyway,' recalls Celia. 'Ossie had said to him, "Why don't you take Celia? She's never been".' 'Celia was a very good observer of people and of street fashion when we were in New York,' says Hockney.

When Hockney was in Britain, he and Celia went to Glyndebourne. 'David loves the opera and theatre and he always goes to them when he's in London,' says Celia. (Hockney would design the sets for a production of Stravinsky's *The Rake's Progress* there in 1975 and Mozart's *The Magic Flute* in 1978, among other operas.) 'A big group of us, including the wife of John Kasmin [Hockney's first dealer] went there in 1970. Quite a few of us drove there from London in a charabanc. David knew the Christies, who ran it, and we were treated very well. Peter Langan [the restaurateur behind fashionable 70s eatery Langan's Brasserie] provided the food. Everyone got very drunk.'

grand tours

That year, Celia also joined Hockney and Schlesinger on a trip to Vittel, in France. "Peter wanted to investigate Europe, and David, who'd spent so much time in L.A., had forgotten how wonderful Europe was. David has a thing about spas—including the one at Vichy—and he wanted to take the waters at Vittel. The water there is very strong and pungent. People drink it for its cleansing properties."

In the spring of 1971, Celia, Hockney, and Peter took off to Marrakech, staying in the swanky Mamounia Hotel. "The hotel was fabulous and very grand," recalls Celia. "We met Kenneth Clark [art critic famous for the 1969 TV series *Civilisation*] on the terrace. Peter was definitely more interested in the social side—he found out where Talitha Getty's home was. David wanted to see the culture. They were often at loggerheads over this when they traveled."

It was here that Celia posed for one of Hockney's iconic ultraromantic, early '70s crayon drawings of her, in a white cotton dress with printed red borders (shown on page 2). A lot of his deliciously delicate crayon portraits of Celia of this period were done in Paris in 1972 and 1973. "Celia is a very good model," says Hockney. "Her face isn't a mask, it reveals a lot. There are many, many faces there."

In the summer of 1971, Celia, pregnant with George, went on holiday to Carennac, in southwest

Opposite above: *Celia, Schlesinger, and Hockney at a party.*
Opposite below: *Celia on holiday in Vittel, France, 1971, photographed by Hockney.*
Above: *Celia at Glyndebourne, 1970, photographed by Schlesinger. Celia often went to see operas there with Hockney.*

France, with Ossie, Hockney, Schlesinger, Mo, George Lawson, Wayne Sleep, and Maurice Payne, an etcher who worked for Hockney. That summer, however, Hockney and Schlesinger split up.

"Ossie and I drove there in his fancy silver Buick," says Celia. "We stayed for about two weeks at a dilapidated, but very grand, chateau in rural France, with *toile de Jouy* wallpapers flaking off the walls, which was rented by Kasmin. His wife, Jane, came, and we were a bit nervous of her then. There was only one bathroom—officially hers. So whenever she went for a swim in the river nearby, we'd all rush in and have a bath. There were a few artists staying, too. Howard Hodgkin was there. Terence and Caroline Conran were also there with their young son, Tom. It was self-catering and quite frantic with all the men showing off about their cuisine. I've got happy memories of it. Mo, whom I was very close with, was always fun to be with. We'd go for walks by the river. I posed for David

in a summer house in the garden, and he did a lovely portrait of me in a vintage dressing gown which I'd probably picked up in Portobello Market."

In 1973, Celia, Ossie, and Hockney went on holiday to San Francisco. "David knew the Rolling Stones, and Ahmet Ertegun [founder of Atlantic Records], who knew the Stones, flew me and the children in a private plane from New York to San Francisco," says Celia. "We stayed in Nob Hill, but I didn't like San Francisco as much as L.A."

Above, clockwise from top left: Celia and Mo McDermott on holiday in Carennac, France; Celia bathing with Mo in the gardens of the chateau rented by Kasmin, Hockney's then dealer; Celia and Ossie at Powis Terrace, snapped by Hockney, 1970; Celia with Schlesinger in Vittel, France, 1971, photographed by Hockney.
Opposite: Celia drawn in crayon by Hockney in the summerhouse in the garden at Carennac, 1971. Celia always chose what to wear when posing for Hockney—in this case a vintage dressing gown.

Overleaf: Celia on holiday in Vittel, France, 1970, photographed by Hockney.

"I drew a lot closer to Celia . . . and started making more drawings of her."

Above: Celia in a Negligée, Paris, *by Hockney, 1971—one of many ultraromantic crayon drawings of Celia done by him in Paris in the early '70s.*
Right: *Celia at Paris restaurant La Closerie des Lilas, circa 1972. She and Hockney loved eating out together in Paris.*

140   Celia Birtwell

"Celia is a very good model.
Her face isn't a mask, it reveals a lot.
There are many, many faces there."

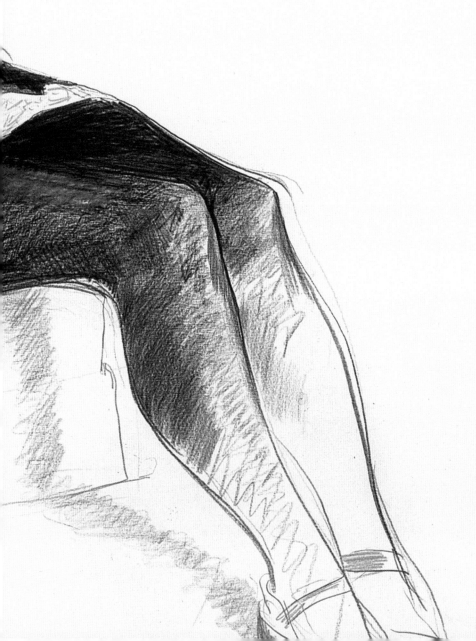

Celia in a Black Slip, Reclining, Paris, *1973,*
a crayon drawing by Hockney. Celia posed in
Tony Richardson's Paris apartment.

Left and above: *Celia in San Francisco, where she went on holiday in 1973 with Hockney—who took both these pictures—and Ossie.*

143

Celia loved trawling through L.A.'s vintage clothing shops, particularly in Melrose, where she bought naval jackets and button-fronted bell-bottoms, as well as the markets at Hollywood Bowl, which sold old furniture and clothes. At the time Celia was hugely into '40s clothes and hats, and liked wearing black—an unusual color to sport in the '70s but one that the decade's arty sophisticates favored. Says Celia:

"I've always loved black because I was a beatnik in Salford."

"That also explains the striped tops I wore in some of Hockney's portraits of me in the '80s. I've always loved sailor suits, which stems from the fact that I really like early Chanel style. I also like plain colors. It's a dichotomy in me that although I design prints, I don't think I do them justice really, though I wore prints a lot for David's portraits."

Celia also loved Pasadena: "I went to the old department stores there. I also liked going to Frederick's of Hollywood and to the Fred Segal shop in L.A. I met fascinationg people through David in L.A, like Billy Wilder. I had dinner at his apartment. It was open-plan but separated into areas by room dividers. He had marvelous food-themed paintings in his dining room, and Picassos. I wanted to talk to him about Marilyn Monroe, but all he would say, sadly, was that she was very difficult."

"David and I rented a big camper van, and traveled to Yosemite, in California, and beyond that to Zion Canyon and Mountain Valley, in Utah," Celia continues. "David didn't trust the van, as it was rather old, and thought it might break down, so he had a friend to drive behind it in case it did. We cheated in a way because the air-conditioning had failed, so we never slept in the van but in motels. We'd listen to Puccini, watch sunsets, go horse-riding. We loved the barren landscapes."

"Towards the end of the holiday, Ossie came to California and we went back to London together."

a bigger splash

Around this time, the life of Hockney and co. in Notting Hill was the subject of the cult film *A Bigger Splash*, released in 1974, in which Celia is shown talking to Hockney as his confidante and cutting Mo McDermott's hair at Linden Gardens. "Cutting hair was one of my favorite hobbies," she says. "It's got nothing to do with the fact I worked at Wig Creations—I used to cut people's hair at art school."

Stills taken from the 1974 movie A Bigger Splash: *Hockney's portrait* Celia in Red and White Dress, *seen in close-up (left);* Celia cutting Mo McDermott's hair at Linden Gardens *(above).*

alternative miss world

A *Bigger Splash* also included footage of an Ossie/Celia catwalk show and the party after the 1972 Alternative Miss World Contest, the anti-beauty pageant, initially held by the sculptor Andrew Logan at his London homes and frequented by the city's avant-garde. Its contestants, dressed in kitsch, over-the-top ensembles, went by such ironic monickers as Miss Crêpe Suzette (Derek Jarman's name as overall winner in 1975), Miss Gale Force Wind and Miss Wolverhampton Baths. Celia was a judge at the 1973 Alternative Miss World (which is still held today), and has been a close friend of Andrew's ever since the two met through Ossie in the early '70s. "I decided I wanted most of the judges to be fashion designers that year," says Andrew. "So they were Celia, Ossie, Zandra Rhodes, Thea Porter, and Barbara Hulanicki, as well as Hockney, Angie Bowie, David Bailey, Molly Parkin, and Amanda Lear." Celia and Hockney were also judges at the 1975 contest. "Celia has always been very loyal to Alternative Miss World," says Logan, beaming. "I think Andrew's Miss Worlds are wonderful," says Celia. "I particularly liked one held on Clapham Common, London, 1978, where a male makeup artist calling himself Miss Linda Carriage rode on stage on a donkey, and the judges appeared in cages so they looked like animals."

"Celia would invite a small gathering around to her place and we'd have wild dancing evenings, dancing to songs like Marvin Gaye's 'I Heard it Through the Grapevine,'" remembers Logan. "I fell in love with Celia's personality: she's very warm, funny, witty. And down-to-earth—I suppose that's a Northern thing."

modeling for hockney

Celia continued to pose often for Hockney in her ultraromantic or vintage clothes. Vintage clothing was suddenly very popular in the '70s both because of major revivals of the 1920s, '30s, and '40s and because

people increasingly wanted to dress in an individual way and so craved one-off pieces. "I was very into vintage lingerie," remembers Celia. "Word spread at the time about a woman who had trunkloads of wonderful '30s negligées which she sold at her home in Fulham."

"Yes, I left it to Celia to decide what to wear in her portraits," says Hockney. "She'd buy these good outfits in Paris. When we went to Vichy, she pointed out all these marvelous old lace knicker [pantie] shops for ladies. I wouldn't have bothered with them, but she showed them to me. So I said get some. They were old, very French, stylish; Celia was very French in the early '70s." But Celia says he never liked her wearing black clothes: "He likes drawing prints and colors."

Celia believes it wasn't just her softly feminine clothes that lent Hockney's portraits of her a romantic air: "David and I became very close after he and Peter split. We were both having a terrible time—he because of Peter, me with Ossie. David really opened his heart to me. We'd have long talks about how he felt. I think when he painted me, he almost saw me in a romantic light. He used to call me names like 'Little Celia.'"

Above: *Miss Gale Force Wind (real name: Burnel Penhaul), winner of the Alternative Miss World, 1991.*
Right: *Celia posing with Logan by her little white Fiat sports car in the '70s.*

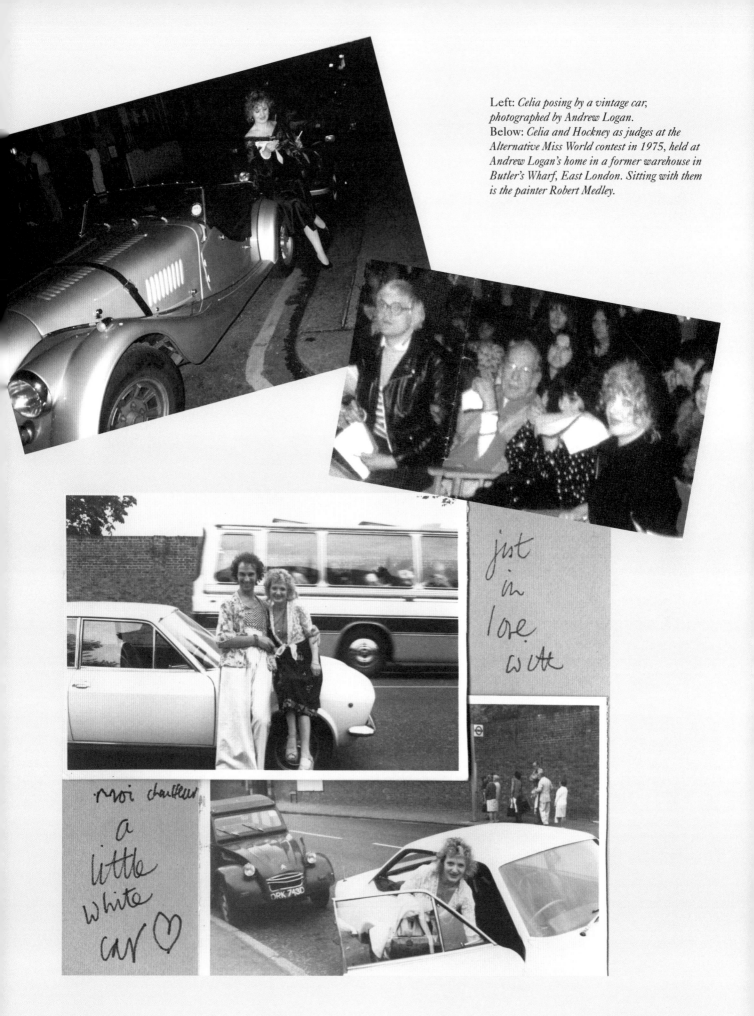

Left: *Celia posing by a vintage car,
photographed by Andrew Logan.*
Below: *Celia and Hockney as judges at the
Alternative Miss World contest in 1975, held at
Andrew Logan's home in a former warehouse in
Butler's Wharf, East London. Sitting with them
is the painter Robert Medley.*

jist
in
love
with

moi chauffeur
a
little
white
car ♥

The portraits of me reflect the fact that we were very close." By about 1973, she says, Hockney was closer to Celia than to Ossie: "When things got very bad with Ossie, he'd say, "You should get away from this, it won't get any better.'"

Not that they chatted while Hockney was drawing or painting her. "He has to have total quiet, no music. His face becomes really contorted with concentration when he draws," says Celia. For posing, Hockney would ask her to sit somewhere, then move around. "I'd keep moving until he'd say, 'Yes, I like that.'" Celia generally poses for two to three hours. "But he takes a break, then I'll have a look at the drawing."

In 1973, Celia, Albert, and George stayed with Hockney in L.A. in a house he had rented in Malibu. "You could go for great walks on the beach there," says Celia. "It's so big you felt like you could walk forever. I witnessed my first earthquake in Malibu. It happened in the middle of the night. There was a definite tremor. David, who'd just been woken up by it, came into my room with his hair standing on end, and said to me, 'Are you all right, luvvie?' It was sweet that he was so concerned."

three rivers

For Hockney, one of their most memorable excursions was to Utah and Nevada in the mid-'80s, which he calls "Three rivers day." "Albert was about 16, George 14, and we had an R.V. [recreational vehicle]," he says. "One morning, the boys wouldn't get up, so I said to Celia, 'Why don't we walk to where the canyon gets very narrow, and you can even wade up the river and be touching both sides of the canyon as it's so narrow. So we waded up the river till it got to near our waists. I knew you shouldn't do it too much because you get these flash floods, but we did. Then we walked

back, and the boys were getting out of bed, so we drove towards L.A. About 40 miles from Zion Canyon, there's a spot where there's a strange spa with a hot pool and a river next to it. A hot-water spring runs into the river so it's warm to swim in. Well, we stopped there and all went swimming in the river with the semiarid desert of Utah around you. This was the second river. Then we're going back to L.A. and the boys say they want to stop in Las Vegas at an aqua park called Wet and Wild. Celia said, 'OK,' so we found it. It's a terrific aqua park with massive chutes. Around its edge was what they called a 'lazy river— water moving slowly in a big circle. I pushed Celia into it, and said, 'Just float and you go under all the bridges, and you keep going round.' So when we were driving back to L.A., I said to Celia, 'Do you realize that within about six hours we were in three different types of river? At 8:30 this morning we were in raw nature, wading up the Virgin River in Zion Canyon. An hour later we were in freaky nature, swimming in a hot river with the grandeur of semiarid nature all around us. Then in Las Vegas we were in another river, high artifice this time, totally false. So when you think about it, Celia, a fantastic combination, and I don't suppose we'll ever be able to repeat this.' And I haven't been able to, I tried to another time with someone else, but I couldn't because the second time the river in Zion Canyon was too ferocious to wade into. But I did notice on the drive back to L.A. just thinking about the day we'd had and how interesting and different each river was."

"It was a very memorable day. It was accidental—not planned."

Above: *Celia's sons Albert and George in Utah on the day of the Three Rivers excursion, 1984, photographed by Celia.*
Opposite: Celia Seated on an Office Chair, *1973, an etching in color by Hockney. Celia sat for him wearing a Chinese silk, floral-patterned kimono-shaped top at Pembroke Studios, his London studio.*

Left: *Celia in 1979 at the lithography studio in L.A. used by Hockney. Sid Felson, who ran the studio, took this picture. Celia wears a scarf featuring one of her prints of the time called Wild.*
Below and right: *Celia photographed by Hockney in California in 1979 beside—and inside— an empty pool whose interior he was painting.*

After Celia's relationship with the artist Adrian George finished in 1978 and she had stopped working for Radley, Hockney offered work as a paid model for about five years. "David invited me to California in 1978," recalls Celia. Around this time, Hockney was painting the inside of a client's swimming pool with his trademark dancing turquoise arcs (visual shorthand for sunlit water), and he photographed Celia (who was then sporting a '50s look: her hair shorter, a compact halo of curls) posing in it, Esther Williams-style. One photo of her taken by him shows her in a '50s dirndl and a plasticised tote bag. "My mother made some plasticized fabric bags, which I sold at various shops," says Celia. "They are the precursors of my vanity cases." At the time, Celia also designed a collection of animal-markings fashion prints called Wild, which later formed the basis of some of her interiors fabric prints.

"I'd be posing for David in L.A. for a couple of weeks a year. I often had the children with me," recalls Celia. "We'd stay at his house in the hills which he initially rented and later bought in 1979."

Celia   Los

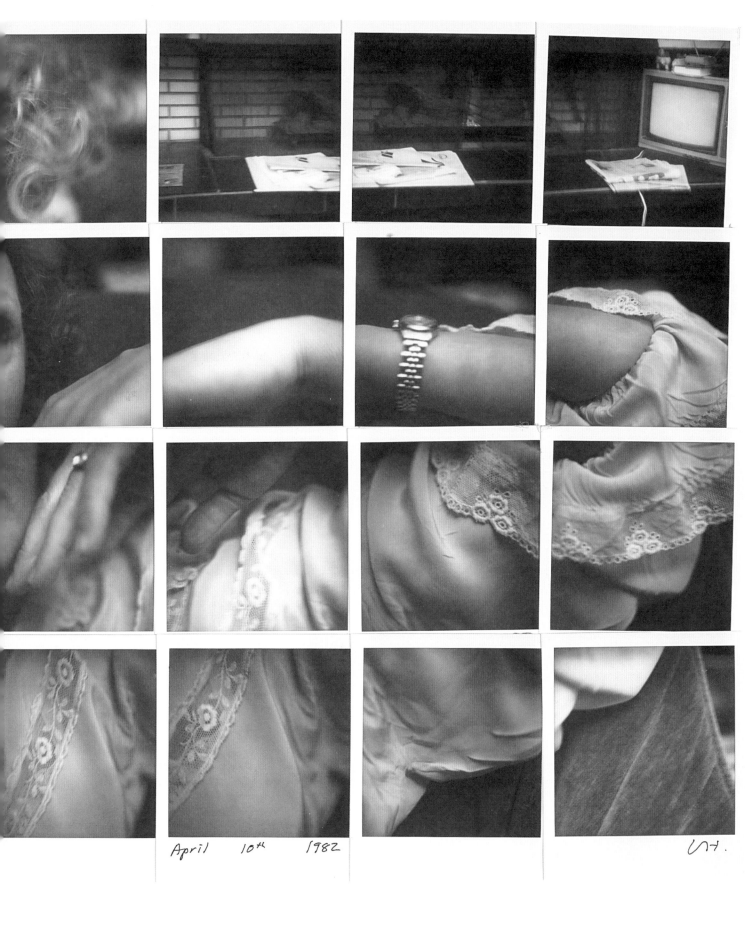

April 10th 1982

Above: Celia, Los Angeles, *1982, one of Hockney's "composite Polaroids," as he calls this '80s series. Celia was wearing a silk and lace, bias-cut Ossie blouse.*

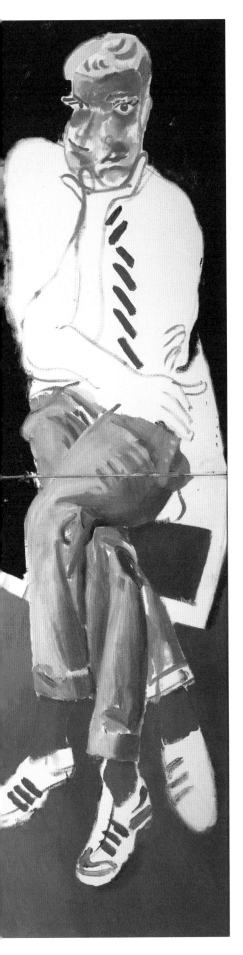

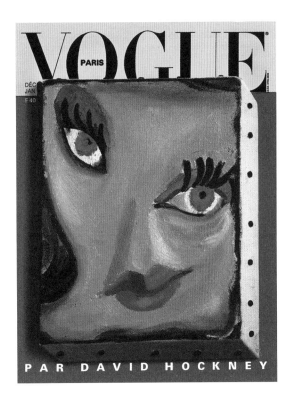

In 1979, in L.A., Celia sat for Hockney for a series of black-and-white, Matisse-influenced lithographs, produced by his L.A. lithography studio, Gemini Gel, run by Sid Felson. With names like *Celia Smoking* and *Celia Elegant*, these had a looser, painterly style, yet looked austere for being monochrome. Celia has two in her house.

In 1982 Celia was the subject of one of Hockney's Polaroid composites, investigations of Cubism and pictorial space, which were exhibited that year in a show in New York called *Drawing with a Camera*. "I'm wearing a very pretty Ossie blouse in it," says Celia. "David also did one—a family portrait of me and the boys and our cat—at Linden Gardens." That year, she also sat for a Hockney four-panel portrait. Hockney's interest in Cubism also manifested itself in his mid-'80s paintings.

Many of his portraits then of Celia resemble Picasso's '30s canvases of his lover Dora Maar.

In 1984, Hockney created a 41-page essay for the December 1985/ January 1986 issue of French *Vogue*, made up of photo collages, drawings, paintings, and his writing. The cover featured a portrait of Celia in a Cubist style.

Left: David, Celia, Stephen, and Ian, *London, 1982, oil on eight canvases, by Hockney. Celia aside, the subjects were David Graves, Hockney's assistant, painter Stephen Buckley, and Ian Falconer, painter, illustrator, and author of the best-selling Olivia children's books.*
Above: *Celia on the cover of the Hockney edition of French* Vogue.

"French *Vogue* held a lunch in a very smart restaurant in celebration of David in Paris, and his mother was there," remembers Celia. "It was very glamorous. I wore a beautiful Ossie black velvet and lace dress. And there was a celebration cake iced with a very impressive copy of that *Vogue* cover portrait of me." Another memory of those times was of David holding a dinner party for Celia and Elizabeth (Wyndham, who worked at Celia's shop) at his home in the hills in 1987. "David designed a lovely invitation for us. Billy Wilder was there, too!"

Another time, Celia and her partner Andrew Palmer, whom she met that year, spent a couple of weeks in David's home in Malibu, off the Pacific Coast Highway. "It was small and made of wood with an outside deck just by the beach," says Celia. "We went on lovely walks, and you could watch the rolling waves. I loved going there. It felt as if it was in a time warp, from a different era. It was previously owned by an elderly photographer and still had the traces of her life there. David had painted his bedroom walls with a faux-wallpaper in purples and blues. He had lots of my fabrics there, too. It was a really wafty, airy seaside house."

A shared interest in aesthetics and a fascination with each other's work and style have drawn Celia and Hockney together. "David thinks I've got a good eye. He respects my taste, style, and work. He'll say about some new print, 'That's good.'" "She developed a style

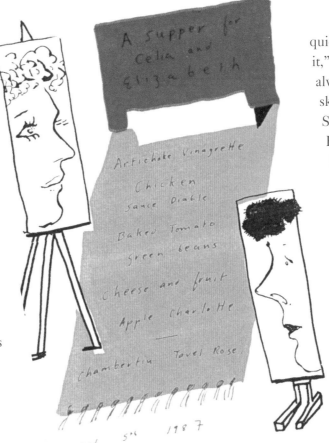

quickly, kept at it, refined it," Hockney says. "I always thought her fashion sketches were very good. She's a very good artist. Her designs are always like her—lively."

"There's a sympathy between us over all things visual," says Celia. "And David is very interested in interiors. For him, it's important that they be comfortable otherwise; they're not doing their job, and that's influenced me and made me more relaxed about my style. The word 'cozy' for him is important: he loves soft carpets and comfy beds."

'For him, it's also about appreciating a bohemian style of life. He hates the way in magazine interiors shoots you never see an ashtray!'

In fact, Hockney's house in Bridlington, Yorkshire, has a 'red room' inspired by one in Celia's London home. It is furnished with many of her fabrics, for example, curtains with her Jacobean print. She also chose a lot of furniture and lamps for his home.

'David's a great host,' Celia says. 'You feel completely at ease. Staying with him is very relaxing and inspiring. He's not at all territorial. He always makes sure there are pretty flowers in your bedroom. You can do what you want, get up when you want, nap when you want. He's very hospitable. Lunch and dinner are important to him. He'll often have several interesting people round for dinner. In Bridlington, we love going for walks on the beach.'

Left: An Image of Celia, *lithograph, screenprint and collage on paper in a hand-painted frame, 1984. A detail of this Cubist-inspired work, showing Celia's face, was featured on the cover of French Vogue, December 1985/January 1986.*
Above: *A menu designed by Hockney for a dinner party he held in 1987 at his home in LA for Celia and Elizabeth Wyndham.*

Celia
at home

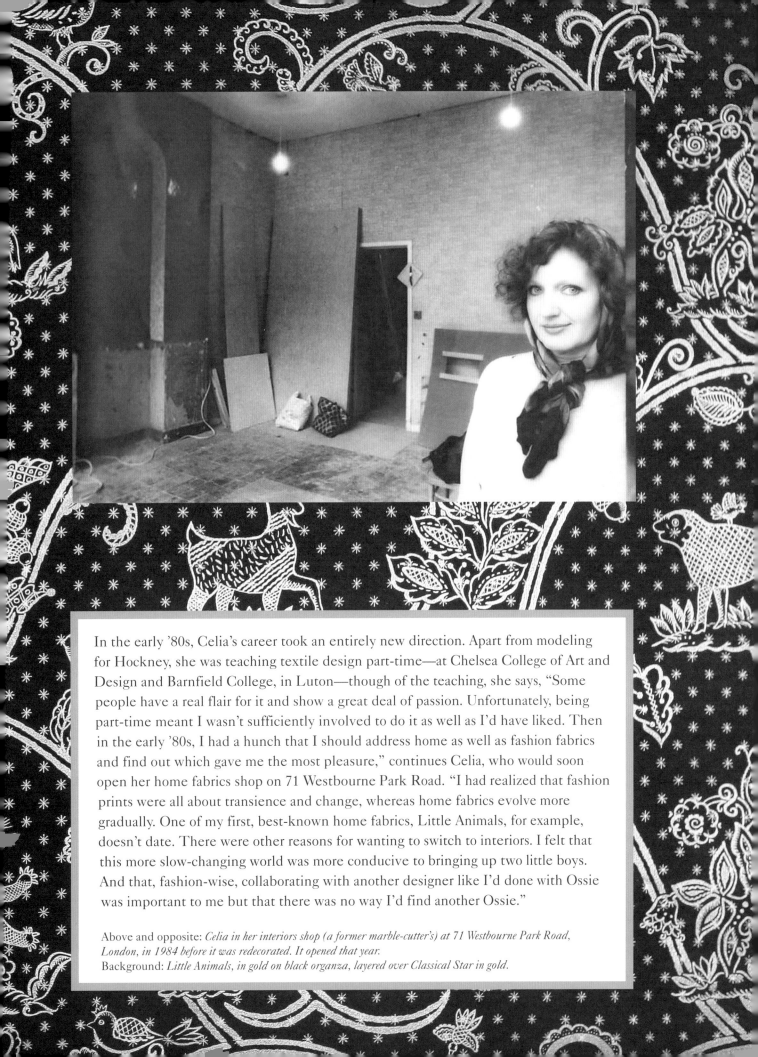

In the early '80s, Celia's career took an entirely new direction. Apart from modeling for Hockney, she was teaching textile design part-time—at Chelsea College of Art and Design and Barnfield College, in Luton—though of the teaching, she says, "Some people have a real flair for it and show a great deal of passion. Unfortunately, being part-time meant I wasn't sufficiently involved to do it as well as I'd have liked. Then in the early '80s, I had a hunch that I should address home as well as fashion fabrics and find out which gave me the most pleasure," continues Celia, who would soon open her home fabrics shop on 71 Westbourne Park Road. "I had realized that fashion prints were all about transience and change, whereas home fabrics evolve more gradually. One of my first, best-known home fabrics, Little Animals, for example, doesn't date. There were other reasons for wanting to switch to interiors. I felt that this more slow-changing world was more conducive to bringing up two little boys. And that, fashion-wise, collaborating with another designer like I'd done with Ossie was important to me but that there was no way I'd find another Ossie."

Above and opposite: *Celia in her interiors shop (a former marble-cutter's) at 71 Westbourne Park Road, London, in 1984 before it was redecorated. It opened that year.*
Background: *Little Animals, in gold on black organza, layered over Classical Star in gold.*

At the time, Celia was selling the plasticized accessories which her mother made out of her designs at her home in Linden Gardens. In early 1984 she found the right premises for her shop. "It was one of two shops that had been a marble-cutter's called Tathams. I chose one where Tatham had sold tiles, partly because it has a lovely floor with a patchwork of different tiles. It didn't have a basement, which would have been useful, but I still loved it. I had just enough money to refurbish it—not in a modern way but keeping it old-fashioned," Celia recalls. "I realized it was essential to have a long counter, which you could measure fabrics on. I wasn't sure how to display the fabrics at the time, but I took inspiration from Liberty, which hung folded bolts of fabric on hangers from a rail." Celia also moved from Linden Gardens to a house opposite the shop. Around this time she met her boyfriend, Andrew, who renovates houses.

The shop opened in November that year. "I didn't have a launch party or anything. It was all very low-key," recalls Celia. "Early on we mainly stocked accessories—my mother's bags, some of my scarves and heart-shaped satin cushions made by Kathleen Coleman. I also designed a matchbox bearing one of my face motifs."

The shop might have opened to no fanfare, but life there never lacked excitement.

This was partly because of the presence of Elizabeth Wyndham, Celia's first employee. "I met her through Mo. She was my bookkeeper-cum-friend-cum-amuser," remembers Celia. "She's Scottish and was briefly married to one of the sons of the rather grand writer Violet Wyndham. Elizabeth chain-smoked these very long cigarettes—king-size Consulates. I was intrigued by the fact that she'd once been a snake charmer in Paris." "I worked there part-time—three days a week," remembers Wyndham.

"I loved working there. I've never laughed so much in all my life."

"And the area was crawling with eccentrics. Antiquarian bookseller David Batterham and Divine [the drag-queen star of many John Waters' movies] were both fans of the shop then."
But while her new incarnation as a home fabric designer was never dull, Celia admits that it wasn't easy to move from fashion to home fabrics. "I had no knowledge of doing furnishing fabrics," she says. "I regretted that I hadn't worked with an interior decorator for a while."

Previous pages: *David Hockney's photocomposite image of the shop window, with Celia's face superimposed on it, commissioned in 1984 by* Harper's & Queen *magazine. Her fabric Bohemian Chintz, created the same year and featuring blown-up paisley motifs, can be seen on two cushions at the far left.*
Fabrics, clockwise from top left: *Trellis, Beasties, Little Animals, Animal Solo, Classical Star, Pembridge Paisley, Animal Trellis, Westbourne Star Stripe, Animal Solo, Pagodas.*

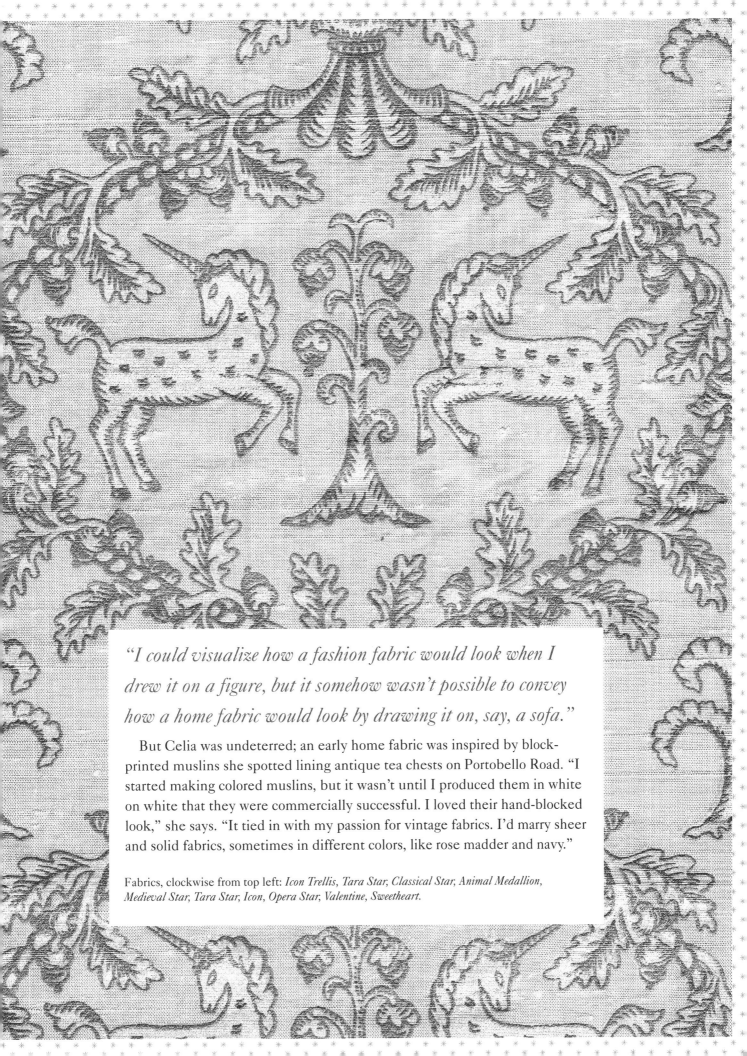

"I could visualize how a fashion fabric would look when I drew it on a figure, but it somehow wasn't possible to convey how a home fabric would look by drawing it on, say, a sofa."

But Celia was undeterred; an early home fabric was inspired by block-printed muslins she spotted lining antique tea chests on Portobello Road. "I started making colored muslins, but it wasn't until I produced them in white on white that they were commercially successful. I loved their hand-blocked look," she says. "It tied in with my passion for vintage fabrics. I'd marry sheer and solid fabrics, sometimes in different colors, like rose madder and navy."

Fabrics, clockwise from top left: *Icon Trellis, Tara Star, Classical Star, Animal Medallion, Medieval Star, Tara Star, Icon, Opera Star, Valentine, Sweetheart.*

Almost her first customer was Norman Bain. "Celia told me she was opening a shop," he recalls. "On the day it opened I turned up nice and early and thought I was going to be her first customer. But as I arrived I saw a man whose car was covered in oil who said he desperately needed to get hold of a rag. I suggested he buy a piece of fabric from Celia's shop, which he did, so I was pipped to the post [beaten to the draw]."

"While Celia and Ossie often worked with soft, diaphanous fabrics, Celia felt at home using thicker, more opaque fabrics like linen and velvet as well. She appeared to make the transition from fashion to interiors easily. She had a good sense of proportion with home fabrics. She knew which prints would look good with curtains as opposed to, say, with cushions. And her home fabrics were as witty as her fashion ones."

Other friends weren't surprised that Celia made the crossover to interiors: "It seemed a natural progression," says Brian Harris.

"Celia had always been a good homemaker. She always made rooms look pretty."

"Back in the '60s, she created stylish interiors with stripped pine floors and, before they became widely popular, large, old office or school clocks hung on the wall."

A very early home fabric was Pretty Roses, which Patrick Procktor bought for some curtains for his home in Manchester Square, London, where he lived until one day a cigarette caused it to go up in flames.

On revisiting one of her favorite sources of inspiration, the V&A, Celia was struck by a framed piece of Jacobean embroidery —the inspiration for Little Animals, which, designed in 1984, features, heraldic-looking beasts like unicorns, porcupines, and lions with sunlike manes.

"I liked the simplicity and slight crudeness of Jacobean embroidery."

"I did lots of drawings from tapestries and embroideries, including medieval ones," says Celia. Her late '60s fashion print Monkey Puzzle had been influenced by similar tapestries.

Little Animals was created with the aid of Ellen Haas at Ivo Printers. "Ellen helped me create the repeat pattern based on my drawings," says Celia. "The airy-fairyness of my ideas needed her talent for precision, her restrictive, economical approach to design. Ellen was technically very clever. This was all the more impressive at a time which predated computers, when we'd have to hang a huge swatch of fabric on the wall to find out if the repeat pattern worked. I liked the movement of Little Animals —the way the animals were embraced by the arabesques framing them. I liked Little Animals so much that two years later I couldn't resist taking them out of this setting and transferring them onto a fabric with a trellis pattern."

Indeed, Little Animals soon spawned an entire family of related designs. "Elizabeth said she preferred the idea of liberating the animals from the trellis framework,

Left: *Celia in her shop, photographed by British* Vogue *(1994).*
Fabrics clockwise from top left: *From Celia's Neptune collection, Tartan, Neptune, Pluto.*

so we tried that," says Celia. "She named it Animal Solo, which I thought was correct and amusing." Another permutation was 1988's Animal Medallion—a mirror image of two prancing unicorns encircled by garlands of oak leaves and acorns.

This family of prints proved very popular. "I think it was because of the English national obsession with animals," ventures Wyndham. According to Celia, the prints have lasted "because the animals aren't cute or twee. Personally, I don't get bored with them." In fact the success of the print has been such that variations resurfaced in years to come with Beasties and Kew (both from 1995) and Birds and Bees (2006), the first two inspired by Kew Gardens, the latter featuring pastels printed on crunchy linens. "Andrew and I became 'Friends of Kew' about 20 years ago, and love watching the seasons change during our weekly visits."

Opposite above: *Celia with her mother in her garden in Salford.*
Opposite below: *Celia photographed by Andrew Logan in Kew Gardens, a perennial inspiration for her designs, such as her fabric Kew* (left).
Above: *Celia's partner, Andrew Palmer, in the hills above Fountains Abbey, Yorkshire.*

Another early design was the exuberant Bohemian Chintz (1984), which, in another echo of her fashion prints, recalled the brio of her print Golden Slumbers. Another print of 1986, Petit Palms, also harks back to her eponymous fashion print. "Bohemian Chintz was based on a traditional chintz but given my spin. It's what I call a 'Birtwelled' chintz," says Celia. "David [Hockney] said it was a witty take on chintz." Indeed, one colorway—in zingy scarlet, jade green, and electric blue—is a far cry from the dusty, fusty palette traditionally associated with chintzes. Similarly vibrant is her print Carnival, of 1986. Featuring carnival masks, its red, gold and green colorway directly referred to the Rastafarian flag and was influenced by the Notting Hill Carnival—yet again, Celia was inspired by her immediate environment.

Soon after, Little Animals, Animal Trellis, Animal Solo, Carnival, Bohemian Chintz, and Pagodas caught the eye of a buyer at Liberty, which sold them under the name "Portobello Collection." Some of the fabrics were also stocked by Harvey Nichols. This collection expanded in the late '80s, and incorporated other designs, such as California, Westbourne Star, and Portobello Paisley. The 1986 print Cat Faces—picturing Celia's trademark faces given a feline twist with slanting eyes, whiskers, and small devilish horns against a kitschy leopard print—was another early design (printed on chiffon and cotton).

notting hill eccentrics

Yet to be gentrified, the area around Westbourne Park Road was peopled by eccentrics who often frequented Celia's shop. Just as Celia gave her fabrics quirky names, so she nicknamed the colorful oddballs who wandered into the shop. While more conventional people might have considered them too antisocial to mix with, Celia didn't turn them away—testament to her bohemian attitude. "There was Mr. Pigeon, who'd appear carrying sacks of grain for the pigeons he kept in his basement," says Celia. "There was The Bearded Lady, a Greek woman called Maria who literally had a beard and a dog called Zob. She'd sit on a wall nearby and knit with one hand using one knitting needle. She stunk to high heaven of pee. Another character used to wheel along a Silver Cross baby pram with her dog in it."

"Yet another oddity," recalls Wyndham, "was Mrs. Poodle. We called her that because she had a poodle named André after André Previn, whom she was a huge fan of. She wore plus-fours and an old-fashioned flying helmet, and was of an indeterminate gender. She looked like a character from Radclyffe Hall's book *The Well of Loneliness*. We were

Background: *The fabric Howard from the Imagine collection.*
Right: *Three pictures of Celia in her shop and* (bottom right) *an interior featuring the Howard fabric, used by interior designer Jenny Armit and featured in the* New York Times.

young and attractive at the time, and I think she liked to come in and feast her eyes on us." "She was a customer of a print dealer called Adam Buck who had a shop called Norman Blackburn on Ledbury Road in Notting Hill, which sold fabulous 18th-century prints of children," elaborates Celia. "Mrs. Poodle got me into these prints; I have one in my house today."

In 1991, Wyndham wanted to leave London, so Celia found a new bookkeeper in Angela Childs. They worked together until 2006. "Angela was very supportive," says Celia.

"At first, I overlapped a bit with Elizabeth, who showed me the ropes," recalls Childs. "She was very funny—very naughty and wry." Childs, too, remembers the eccentrics dropping by, some simply "amazed at how artistically the shop had been decorated . . . It was like a soap opera there. There was a woman who walked around holding a huge umbrella in all weathers. There was a 90-year-old man who shuffled past. We'd tease Celia that he was her boyfriend." "He was called Fred, and I nicknamed him Edward Lear because he looked like him," says Celia. "I've always loved Lear—my father bought me his *A Book of Nonsense* when I was about 10. Fred had a sweet face and would always go into the local bookies'. He was always laden with shopping bags, and one day I bought him a buggy to wheel his stuff about in, but he found that really insulting."

"Celia felt sorry for these lame ducks," remembers Childs. "She was very kind to all of them, including The Bearded Lady, who was, frankly, an embarrassment because she stank the shop out," says Wyndham. "But Celia never threw her out. In fact, Celia is probably

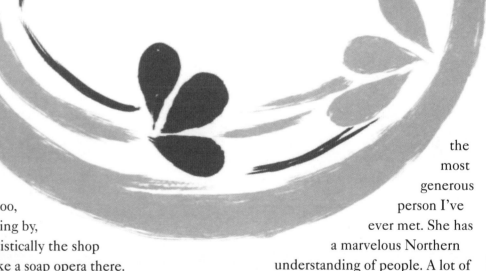

Celia's Imagine collection. The large motif (below) *is taken from one of its fabrics, Olympia.*

the most generous person I've ever met. She has a marvelous Northern understanding of people. A lot of people in southern England are rather cool, but Celia wears her emotions on her sleeve. And this generosity includes material things. Whenever she designed new scarves, she'd say to me, 'Pick one of them.'" "People loved Celia, and she was very giving," concurs Childs. "We had to stop her from giving fabrics away sometimes." Wyndham, meanwhile, remembers that Celia was very maternal toward her sons, who frequently came into the shop: "She loved the boys; she was always very good to them."

But the genial, bohemian insouciance of life at 71 Westbourne Park Road gradually gave way to a more businesslike approach. Childs introduced a no-smoking regime. "The white-on-white fabrics were becoming tarnished, so I implemented a ban," she says. According to Wyndham, the bad image projected

175

Celia Birtwell

by the sight of Nicotine-stained fabrics alone warranted this; moreover, "All these snooty buyers who came in from posh department stores didn't like the fabrics smelling of fags." Business received another boost when Celia met the PR officer Sahra Gott, who strongly recommended that she show at the London, high-end design fair Decorex International. "Meeting Celia was a total fluke," remembers Gott, who knew Ian Thompson, who was Decorex's managing director. "We met in 1990 at the same hairdresser's and, when I got chatting, I asked Celia why she didn't show at Decorex. She said that there was a huge waiting list. So I nipped upstairs and phoned Ian and told him who I was with."

"Celia, in my opinion, is the most talented textile designer in the U.K."

"I said this, and Ian replied that he'd be delighted if Celia showed that September."

For Celia, this was a step up from having occasionally exhibited at Olympia [exhibition hall] in the late '80s, when, with Elizabeth and Duggie Heard (a part-time employee in the '80s), Celia unceremoniously stuffed her car with fabrics and transported them there. Celia showed at Decorex for 10 years, and always referred to Sahra as her "fairy godmother," it made a huge difference to her career. "Decorex introduced Celia's collection to the international market. It was a fantastic showcase for her," says Gott.

At Decorex in 1990, Celia launched her Wild collection—African-inspired animal-print designs in scorched-earth browns, sandy beiges, and rusts, which designer Nicky Haslam nicknamed her "Poor collection." The good-humored Celia didn't begrudge him that but found it funny: "I suppose he said that because it was very abstract and not flowery, unlike anything else at Decorex."

Key to the success of stands at Decorex is their design. Celia went to a lot of trouble with hers, often codesigning them with Philip Prowse. "Philip suggested that the second one, which had a Turkish theme and was inspired by Delacroix, simulate the interior of my shop. It had a bright blue ceiling in a color by (paint brand) John Oliver called Betty Blue," recalls Celia. The stand, with its 19th-century Orientalist look, principally showcased Celia's new, 1991, Cinderella collection. One of its designs, Classical Star—small gold stars studding different colored plain backgrounds, from cream to crimson—was printed on silk douppions.

"One stand had a Turkish theme and was inspired by Delacroix."

This page: The fabric Orphée, also from the Imagine collection, whose images are partly inspired by Jean Cocteau's 1949 film Orphée.

It was meteorically successful and spawned a constellation of related prints, some with punning names: Tara Star (a favorite of Celia's and incorporating rhythmic squiggles), Medieval Star, Movie Star. . . "Classical Star was so popular that at one point it was the mainstay of the business," says Celia. Also gracing the stand was the print Seraglio (from a collection called Neptune and featuring broad stripes), covering a daybed fit for an Ingres odalisque.

"Decorex was very good for me commercially," says Celia. "Sundays were particularly good with European and U.S. buyers. We met the American agent Christopher Hyland there. He took us on and distributed my fabrics in New York. Classical Star was a huge hit there. An organza version, used for what Americans call 'table-top' dressing—fabric laid like a skirt over a table—was particularly sought after. The Conran Shop in London, Paris, and Tokyo also sold the star-pattern fabrics, including one in white on white."

celia's home

Opposite: Celia's drawing room, which she calls "The Red Room." The sofa is covered by her broad-striped fabric Seraglio. There are also sculptures by Brian Harris and Mo McDermott.
Above: A corner of the same room with a chair covered in the print Olympia on linen.

Overleaf, clockwise from left: Celia's hallway; a corner of the dining-room mantelpiece, plates by Piero Fornasetti; a lamp base made of plaster poodles; a photo of Celia's "all-time favourite girl," Marilyn Monroe; chairs in the conservatory upholstered with Isabella fabric.

The witty, playful, lighthearted spirit of Celia's designs is mirrored by the chic, informal style of her Notting Hill home. (Celia and Andrew moved into this two-bedroom, high-ceilinged, Victorian house in 1997.) Ever the Francophile, Celia has given it a stylishly Parisian look. "I like well-proportioned rooms and ornament in the form of old-fashioned windows and fireplaces," she says. The first-floor dining room, with its large windows with wooden shutters, is painted an airy white, as are the adjoining kitchen and conservatory. The latter has French windows leading to her garden, which is filled with scented jasmine and roses. "I like gardens to be perfumed," she continues. "I like drawing flowers in my sketchbooks here. These often form the basis for my floral dress fabrics. There's nothing better than looking at nature. Flowers, for example, are all different, so they always surprise you." In the house itself, vases filled with cut flowers enhance this romantic mood.

But, as her home demonstrates, Celia loves kitsch and artifice, as well as nature. A fan of the artist Joseph Cornell, she has wall-hung cabinets stuffed with curios

bought on her travels or from car-trunk sales held near her second home, a cottage in Shropshire: Mexican Day of the Dead figurines, masks of Disney's Snow White (also from Mexico), silver foil-wrapped Easter bunnies, and lamps made of plaster poodles.

Celia's love of bold color also manifests itself—in her second-floor drawing room, which she calls "The Red Room" because its walls, which teem with paintings, are scarlet. "Red is a great backdrop for art," she says. "Auction houses often display art on walls in bright colors. People are far too scared of color." In the Red Room there's also Natalie Gibson's vibrantly colorful print of her famous cats. The mantelpiece and huge mirror are framed by a funky rope light illuminated at all times of the day. "I always like big mirrors because they're such a great way of creating the impression of more light and space," says Celia.

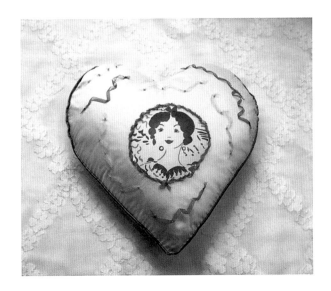

mademoiselle

Celia has often felt that home textiles can be rather bland and are in need of some wit and humor. She came up with her collection of prints called Mademoiselle, which harked back to the faces in her original fashion sketches. The design idea was inspired by Disney's *Snow White* (a film Celia loves) and the arrival of her first granddaughter, Isabella—the name of one of these prints. Others were called Opera House (on red velvet) and Twinkle. Celia also based some scarves on this theme. At one point, she invented a new female character to accompany Mademoiselle, whom she called Mademoiselle's Best Friend, which resulted in a new design that graced one of her scarves.

Opposite, clockwise from top: *The designs Mademoiselle, Twinkle, and Isabella, from the Mademoiselle fabric collection.*
Above: *A heart-shaped cushion featuring an Isabella motif and decorated with ribbons and bows by Kay Dimbleby.*
Below: *A detail from the Mademoiselle fabric, which Celia calls Bouquets.*

clients and fans

A devotee of Celia's is British fashion stylist Liz Thody. "The first fabric I bought from Celia was Beasties, printed in navy on natural linen," says Thody. "I loved the slightly medieval first impression, which on closer inspection was so whimsical and charming. My favorite-ever Celia fabric—now regrettably discontinued—was called Pom-pom. It was a melon-sized, fuzzy-edged spot. I bought it in chocolate brown on camel velvet. I think Celia sold me the last batch and gave me a sausage-dog draft excluder to match [made by Celia's mother]. Her designs are so playful, her palette tasteful, yet somehow she injects into her work a girlishness which is anything but sugary."

High-profile British clients early in this period included interior designers John Stefanidis and David Mlinaric. "Celia Birtwell's designs are unique—unmistakable for their wit and originality. They're as charming and give as much pleasure as the designer herself does in life," comments Stefanidis today.

Celia's fabrics also went down well in France, Belgium, the Netherlands, and Sweden. She was championed particularly by Swedish interior designer Annie Schierenbeck, a business relationship that entailed a glamorous trip one year to Drottningholm Palace, in Sweden. "There were definitely perks to the job, like the Drottningholm trip," remembers Childs. "One year we went to [arts festival] the Paris Biennale; it was also an honor to visit Hockney's studio in London."

The owl and the pussycat
Went to sea
Now the owl has come back
And he's looking at me

Our beautiful songbird
Gets ready to fly
And soon he'll be singing
High up in the sky

A great big pigeon
Walks up the lane
But the farmer won't like him
For he'll eat all his grain

These wise old owls
Are sitting quite mute
When they've finished their thinking
They'll give us a hoot

Look at the Jackal
Quite still don't you feel?
But his eyes must keep watchful
For the chance of a meal

This butterfly's watching
The little bird's legs
"Keep going young birdie
Don't eat all my eggs"

Here's a bright pheasant
Golden and red

The owl and the pussycat
Went to sea

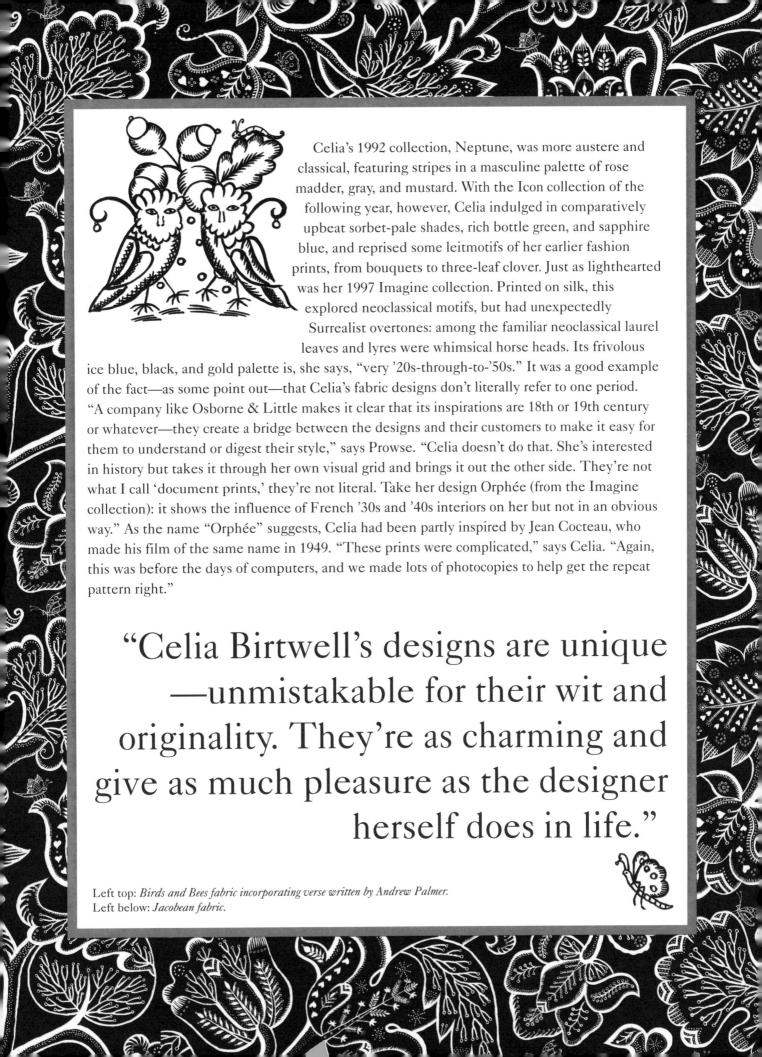

Celia's 1992 collection, Neptune, was more austere and classical, featuring stripes in a masculine palette of rose madder, gray, and mustard. With the Icon collection of the following year, however, Celia indulged in comparatively upbeat sorbet-pale shades, rich bottle green, and sapphire blue, and reprised some leitmotifs of her earlier fashion prints, from bouquets to three-leaf clover. Just as lighthearted was her 1997 Imagine collection. Printed on silk, this explored neoclassical motifs, but had unexpectedly Surrealist overtones: among the familiar neoclassical laurel leaves and lyres were whimsical horse heads. Its frivolous ice blue, black, and gold palette is, she says, "very '20s-through-to-'50s." It was a good example of the fact—as some point out—that Celia's fabric designs don't literally refer to one period. "A company like Osborne & Little makes it clear that its inspirations are 18th or 19th century or whatever—they create a bridge between the designs and their customers to make it easy for them to understand or digest their style," says Prowse. "Celia doesn't do that. She's interested in history but takes it through her own visual grid and brings it out the other side. They're not what I call 'document prints,' they're not literal. Take her design Orphée (from the Imagine collection): it shows the influence of French '30s and '40s interiors on her but not in an obvious way." As the name "Orphée" suggests, Celia had been partly inspired by Jean Cocteau, who made his film of the same name in 1949. "These prints were complicated," says Celia. "Again, this was before the days of computers, and we made lots of photocopies to help get the repeat pattern right."

"Celia Birtwell's designs are unique —unmistakable for their wit and originality. They're as charming and give as much pleasure as the designer herself does in life."

Left top: *Birds and Bees fabric incorporating verse written by Andrew Palmer.*
Left below: *Jacobean fabric.*

By now Notting Hill in general, was changing dramatically, as was the area around the shop—thanks partly to the opening in the mid-'90s of two fashionable institutions: Tom Conran's restaurant The Cow and the revamped gastropub The Westbourne. "In the early '80s, the area had seemed remote, a backwater," remembers artist Belinda Cadbury. "Before it was tarted up [remodeled], the Westbourne had been a rowdy watering hole full of shouting drunks." According to Childs, when the area changed, Celia's shop began attracting "younger, trendier customers. Celia latched on to this change and started creating prints and colors in a more fun way. People bought fabrics for their children's nurseries. Celia's clients were generally well-off. Many came back for more fabrics whenever they bought a new house."

"Then there were younger customers who'd just buy cushions in the star-print fabrics, for example, so they could have a bit of Birtwell at an affordable price."

And, with the '70s revival of the late '90s and noughties, the names Celia Birtwell and Ossie Clark resurfaced. For example, the shop Rellik, a mecca for finger-on-the-pulse fashionistas on Golborne Road, was selling original Celia/Ossie dresses at a time when hipsters and designers were rediscovering pattern, color, and decoration. In 1998, Gott introduced Celia to Phil Cadel, then the managing director of Zoffany, for which Celia did a collection of furnishing designs featuring roses and stripes.

In recent years, Celia's fabrics have included the popular, boldly large-scale design Jacobean, of 2006—a throwback to her earlier interest in Jacobean embroidery. That year, Celia reprised the theme of animals with her faux-naif print Birds and Bees, whose rhymes, in a copperplate script, were written by Andrew.

"I like the way that in the interiors world designers can revisit motifs, and their work can evolve gradually, which you can't do so much in fashion," Celia says.

Never one to let things drift, Celia decided in 2006 that a younger team was needed to run the business. Fortunately, her son George and his wife, Bella, proved to be just the combination and, as Celia wished, would keep the business in the family. George had worked with Celia on several projects over the years, and Bella, a film production manager, was looking for new challenges. They have learned the ropes and given the company a professional makeover. With Celia still ready to give her artistic input, assisted by designer Daniel Croyle and his knowledge of textiles and technical wizardry, and the new team's drive and understanding of technology and marketing, the Celia Birtwell brand is in good hands.

Left: *Bird Song fabric* (above) *and Milson ticking fabric* (below).

Page numbers in italic refer to illustrations

picture credits

41, 63, 70-71, 72, 74-75, 80-81, 91, 92, 98, 104-105, 110, 112, Ken Adlard; 1, 23 (below) 38-39, 76-77, 78-79, 102-103 Ken Adlard, courtesy Shikasuki.

76 Clive Arrowsmith/Vogue © The Condé Nast Publications Ltd.

4 right, 21, 30-31 Norman Bain © Victoria and Albert Museum, London.

78 photograph by Cecil Beaton.

4, 7, 10-11, 12-13, 14 below left and right, 15, 16, top right, 17, 22, 23 top , 24-25, 33 right, 36, 45, 46, 49, 58-59, 60-61, 62, 64-65, 68-69, 70 (left) , 77 (below), 82 ,86 (left and below) , 88-89, 90, 94-95, 96-97, 104, 105, 111 top right and below right, 113, 115 below right, 134 top left, top right, 146, 149, 150 top left, 160, 161, 164, 165, 166, 167, 170 top, 171, 172 , 174-175, 176, 182-183, 184-185, 186-187 courtesy Celia Birtwell.

16 below © Peter Blake. All rights reserved, DACS 2011.

33 top right and below, 80, top, middle and below, 81 middle, 145 top right and left © Buzzy Enterprises Ltd.

83 top and below Stanley Devon/The Sunday Times/ NI Syndication.

77 top right, 108 below © Johnny Dewe Mathews.

35 photograph by Duffy for Nova Magazine.

27, 28, 53, 108 middle © Getty Images.

42 Annette Green/Vogue © The Condé Nast Publications Ltd.

2, 5 left, 77 top, 84, 85, 118, 120, 122-123, 124-125, 126, 127, 132 below, 134 below left and below right, 135, 136-137 , 138, 140-141, 142, 143, 144-145, 148, 150 below, 151, 152-153, 154, 156, 157, 162-163 © David Hockney; 128-129 © David Hockney/ Tate Gallery, London; 155 David Hockney © Vogue Paris.

173 middle, inside back cover by Andrew Lamb

93 Barry Lategan/Vogue ©The Condé Nast Publications Ltd.

111 photograph by Emma Lee (emmaleephotographer.com).

44, 56-57 photographs by Jim Lee © all rights reserved.

50, 73 Lichfield/Condé Nast Archive, © Condé Nast.

147, 170 below, Andrew Logan.

14 top © The Lowry Collection, Salford.

5 middle, 115 top left, 173 top, below left, 178, 179, 180, 181 © Ray Main/Mainstream Images.

168 Robin Matthews/Vogue ©The Condé Nast Publications Ltd.

29 top, 48, 52, 79, 87 David Montgomery/Vogue © The Condé Nast Publications Ltd.

43, 55, 66, 67, 100-101 © Norman Parkinson, Courtesy Norman Parkinson Archive.

115 below left Andrew Palmer.

108 top Patrick Procktor.

40 © Michael Putland/Retna UK .

70, 71, 109 © Rex Features Ltd.

74, 75, 99, 103, 106, 119, 121, 130, 131, 133, 139 © Peter Schlesinger.

14 (frame) www.shutterstock.com

26 Marilyn Stafford, Camera Press, London; 132 top left Marilyn Stafford/Vogue ©The Condé Nast Publications Ltd.

114 top left and below right courtesy of Topshop.

29 below, 34, 38 © Victoria and Albert Museum, London.

16 top left © Michael Ward/National Portrait Gallery, London.

114 below left WENN.

173 below left © The Interior Archive/photograph by Edina van der Wyck/Designed by Jenny Armit.

acknowledgments

I would like to thank everyone who has worked on or contributed to the creation of this book of my life in design, in particular Daniel Croyle, whose unwavering perseverance has guided me through some of the more challenging creative moments, and Bella Clark, Karen Cazabon, Sahra Gott, Dominic Lutyens, and Andrew Palmer who were also vital contributors through their diligence, support, and constant uncovering of new material.

To all my friends, family, work colleagues, mentors and pillars of inspiration; I would like to thank you for the time you have shared with me over the years, whether it has been through being interviewed for the book, scouring your archives for new material, working with me on fashion or home or spending time laughing and chatting. For their contributions to this book thanks go to: Norman Bain, Pattie Boyd, Gay and Dick Brown, Belinda Cadbury, Angela Childs, Albert Clark, George Clark, Luckie Clark, Kathleen Coleman, Vanessa Denza, Fran Findlater, Judith Found, Adrian George, Natalie Gibson, Ellen Haas, Brian Harris, Ray Harris, Nick and Wendy Haywood, David Hillman, David Hockney, Katie Horwich, Andrew Logan, Frances Lynn, David Newell, Molly Parkin, Philip Prowse, Peter Schlesinger, John Stefanidis, Caroline and Derek Todd, Linda Watson, Jon Wealleans, Robert Whitaker, Elizabeth Wyndham.

Celia Birtwell

Editorial Director **Anne Furniss**
Creative Director **Helen Lewis**

Editor **Sarah Mitchell**
Design **Daniel Croyle, Lucy Gowans, Helen Lewis**
Picture research **Katie Horwich**
Editorial assistance **Louise McKeever**
Production **Vincent Smith, James Finan**

CELIA BIRTWELL.
Text, design and layout © 2011 Celia Birtwell/Quadrille Publishing Ltd
Illustrations © 2011 Celia Birtwell
All rights reserved.

Library of Congress Cataloging-in-Publication Data Available Upon Request

ISBN 978-1-250-00306-5

First U.S. Edition: October 2011

10 9 8 7 6 5 4 3 2 1

For information, address St. Martin's Press, 175 Fifth Avenue, New York, N.Y. 10010.

www.stmartins.com

Printed in China.